BRARY
TEER
TO LIBRARY
ADVOCATE

Tapping into the Power of Community Engagement

Carla Campbell Lehn

LIBRARIES UNLIMITED™
An Imprint of ABC-CLIO, LLC
Santa Barbara, California • Denver, Colorado

Library of Congress Cataloging-in-Publication Data

Names: Lehn, Carla Campbell, author.
Title: From library volunteer to library advocate : tapping into the power of community engagement / Carla Campbell Lehn.
Description: Santa Barbara, California : Libraries Unlimited, an imprint of ABC-CLIO, LLC, [2018] | Includes bibliographical references and index.
Identifiers: LCCN 2018005115 (print) | LCCN 2018020676 (ebook) | ISBN 9781440856716 (ebook) | ISBN 9781440856709 (paperback : acid-free paper)
Subjects: LCSH: Volunteer workers in libraries—United States. | Libraries and community—United States. | Libraries—Public relations—United States.
Classification: LCC Z682.4.V64 (ebook) | LCC Z682.4.V64 L44 2018 (print) | DDC 021.20973—dc23
LC record available at https://lccn.loc.gov/2018005115

ISBN: 978-1-4408-5670-9 (paperback)
978-1-4408-5671-6 (ebook)

22 21 20 19 18 1 2 3 4 5

This book is also available as an eBook.

Libraries Unlimited
An Imprint of ABC-CLIO, LLC

ABC-CLIO, LLC
130 Cremona Drive, P.O. Box 1911
Santa Barbara, California 93116-1911
www.abc-clio.com

This book is printed on acid-free paper ∞

Manufactured in the United States of America

Portions of this book are quoted and adapted with permission from: "Volunteer Involvement in California Libraries: Best Practices," Carla Campbell Lehn. Sacramento, CA: California State Library, 1999. Available online at https://getinvolvedclearinghouse.org/resource/training-materials/volunteer-involvement-california-libraries-best-practices; "Get Involved: Library Volunteer Program Improvement Model." Sacramento, CA: California State Library. Available online at https://getinvolvedclearinghouse.org/resource/training-materials/library-volunteer-program-improvement-model; "Get Involved Initiative," Transforming Life after 50. Available online at transforminglifeafter50.org/innovators/get-involved-initiative; and "Volunteer Engagement Course," Transforming Life after 50. Available online at transforminglifeafter50.org/tools-ideas/volunteers/volunteer-engagement-course.

Contents

Preface

WHY THIS COULD WORK FOR YOU: CALIFORNIA'S EXPERIENCE

"Get Involved: Powered by Your Library," a statewide volunteerism initiative of the California State Library, was unveiled in late 2008, during the worst recession since the Great Depression. The national economic disaster created a crisis for libraries, as it did for most public and not-for-profit organizations—less funding, fewer staff, and an increased demand for services.

Libraries were being asked to serve hundreds of new library users by accommodating people who could no longer afford Internet at home; assisting job seekers—many of whom had never touched a mouse before—apply for a job online; and circulating many more books, DVDs, and other materials that were no longer able to be accommodated in the household budgets of many community members.

The Get Involved initiative trained libraries in new approaches to volunteer engagement, including skilled volunteerism, and how to add online sources to a mix of volunteer recruitment strategies through a partnership with VolunteerMatch.org.

California's Get Involved initiative was designed to:

- Raise public library awareness about the benefits of volunteer "engagement"—an updated approach from the traditional volunteer "management" model.
- Assist public libraries in recruiting and engaging high-skilled volunteers.
- Build public library capacity to engage more volunteers, and through this process, develop more library supporters and advocates.
- Position public libraries as centers for civic engagement.

Through the Get Involved initiative, a growing resource has been brought to the library table—high-skilled, high-impact volunteers. Although volunteers can never replace the work of library staff, engagement of more and higher skilled volunteers has aided libraries in enhancing or expanding services to meet user needs. Libraries have successfully recruited for a multitude of skilled volunteer positions including event planner, photographer, graphic designer, homework club coordinator, and public relations specialist, to name a few.

In the first five years of the Get Involved initiative, California's libraries experienced a 52 percent increase in volunteers as measured by the annual statewide library survey and found that 79 percent of these new volunteers were volunteering for a library for the very first time. Both of those statistics were encouraging as they pointed to the fact that new community members were being attracted to the library.

But increasing numbers wasn't the only goal of the initiative—we were also interested in seeing if volunteering for the library could be viewed as a gateway for increased connection to the library.

More than 500 California library volunteers recruited through the Get Involved initiative between July 1, 2012, and June 30, 2016, returned surveys and reported the following when asked how their volunteer experience led to other forms of library support:

- Sixty-six percent had told friends about what the library has to offer.
- Thirty-four percent had introduced friends to volunteer opportunities at the library.
- Seven percent gave money to support the library, and 5 percent asked friends to give.
- Six percent attended a meeting or rally in support of the library.
- Eight percent individually spoke to one or more local decision makers on behalf of the library.

Looking at the data it was evident that if 76 percent of these new volunteers had never volunteered for a library before, and 66 percent of them were out talking to their friends about what the library had to offer, we are already reaching a huge group of people with information about the library beyond those we were able to reach before. And even though asking them to give money to the library, or asking others to do so, was not part of our volunteer engagement initiative, a significant number of volunteers were naturally so inclined.

The survey also contained open-ended questions. Included below are two of them, with just a sampling of volunteer responses:

"Is there something you learned about libraries that surprised you?"

- I am amazed at the vast programs the library offers to the public free of charge. This library is no longer a place just to pick out a book, but a place for early childhood enrichment, school age programs, travel, and literature lectures, etc.

- They offer so many useful, and free, services for the community that more people should take advantage of.

"*How has your experience volunteering in a library helped you understand the changing role of libraries in the community?*"

- Libraries have kept up with technology and yet still have resources available for those who are not tech savvy.
- They're really more than what most people think a library is. It's a community center or even a technology center, and they serve so many people with, sometimes, very little resources.

The insights provided by survey respondents demonstrate that their understanding of the library's role in the community has changed as a result of their volunteer activity. Because these are some of the key messages that libraries want to get out into the community, and because a large percentage of the volunteers are telling their friends about what they've learned—even recruiting friends for volunteer positions at the library—we can demonstrate that volunteers naturally do gravitate to the community ambassador role.

Strategies encouraged by the Get Involved initiative have not only increased the number of volunteers involved in libraries, but also demonstrated volunteers' increased support for the library beyond their volunteer assignment. Recruiting them to do volunteer work that engages their skills and interests, and making them part of the library family, is quite naturally turning them into some of the library's strongest ambassadors, supporters, and advocates.

California's Get Involved initiative is the subject of the chapter entitled "Leading Big Volunteer Operations" in the 2015 book *Volunteer Engagement 2.0: Ideas and Insights Changing the World.*[1]

In 2014, a planning grant from the Institute of Museum and Library Services allowed three additional states to work with California to determine if the Get Involved initiative was replicable in other states. The team enthusiastically embraced the initiative and the possibility of replication, and developed a matrix of "Possible Scalable Approaches for Successful Replication by States" (see table at end of Preface).

The matrix identifies "success factors" for replication of the Get Involved initiative, and in an attempt to make it replicable for states of all sizes, with a variety of staffing and funding capabilities, it details the level of commitment a state would need to make to each success factor in order to achieve "maximum results," "great results," or "good results" for volunteer engagement efforts for libraries in their states.

Later, the state library agencies of Arizona, California, Idaho, and Texas formed a Get Involved Collaborative and were fortunate to receive a three-year grant from the Institute for Museum and Library Services' Laura Bush

21st Century Librarian Program to test implementation of the "maximum," "great" and "good" approaches.

As of this writing, the collaborative project is in its second year, providing good, great, or maximum levels of training and support to libraries in their states. Their second target audience is other state libraries, with whom results will be shared. The project has potential for broad national significance if the matrix can be demonstrated to assist states to increase library volunteerism.

SUMMARY

Many libraries offer "traditional" volunteer jobs only—book shelver, book mender, and shelf duster. Unfortunately, those jobs have limited appeal to today's volunteer. Although some will continue to volunteer for those tasks, others see themselves sharing their expertise, and have a host of skills they are willing to share.

To attract these volunteers and turn them into a natural support system for the library, traditional volunteer programs will need to retool their approach using researched success strategies for volunteer engagement.

Libraries can and should be using volunteer service as a strategy for community engagement. When successfully engaged, many volunteers naturally become library supporters and advocates. People who feel part of the library family, who understand its issues, and understand the important role it plays in the community, will advocate for it, promote it, and help to recruit both financial and human resources.

The techniques and skills shared in this book can help your library achieve these successes. New library volunteers can be counted on to develop additional commitments to the library as ambassadors, supporters, and advocates.

If you think these successes are only possible in a big state like California and couldn't be replicated in your city, county, or rural library community, please think again. Literally hundreds of libraries of all sizes in four states are as of this writing actively engaged in applying the concepts in this book in their own local communities.

A couple of small libraries in Texas have recently inspired me. The director of a library with a service population of 5,000 confessed that she is "IT challenged," so she posted her need for a skilled computer volunteer on VolunteerMatch. Within two weeks she got a call from a man and his partner new to the community who were opening an IT support business there. He had seen her need when the LinkedIn/VolunteerMatch partnership offered it up to him and couldn't wait to get started. They now troubleshoot the computers at the library every other week for 2 hours, and patrons are commenting on the improvement. Now that the library is receiving a grant-funded maker space, these two skilled volunteers have also volunteered to help redesign the space for the equipment's use and storage.

The director of a Texas library serving about 20,000 people needed a logo for a new special project and found a skilled graphic designer on VolunteerMatch living in Pennsylvania who did a beautiful job as a "virtual" volunteer. Without them ever meeting, the volunteer produced the perfect logo and even went farther to develop complementary images that could be used on additional print and online pieces created for the project.[2]

Sometimes small or rural communities believe these resources don't exist where they live. Using the techniques recommended in this book, and reaching out through online recruitment, can help to find local people you didn't know were there or even people far away who are happy to share their skills.

NOTES

1. Rosenthal, Robert J., Ed., *Volunteer Engagement 2.0: Ideas and Insights Changing the World* (Hoboken, NJ: Wiley & Sons, 2015).

2. These two small Texas libraries' stories are featured in a 1-hour archived webinar called "From Management to Engagement: Skilled Volunteers in Public Libraries," which can be viewed here: http://getinvolvedclearinghouse.org/resource/training-materials/management-engagement-skilled-volunteers-public-libraries (accessed November 12, 2017).

Get Involved: Powered by Your Library—Possible Scalable Approaches for Successful Replication by States

Success Factors	For Maximum Results	For Great Results	For Good Results
Secure State Library Management Support	State librarian supports and provides high level of resources such as: Cheerleading and encouragement State staff support Full funding of training/travel and VolunteerMatch premium accounts for all public libraries Models volunteer engagement at the state library Speak about it often at events. Gather other partners (i.e., state service commission and state's library association).	State librarian willing to support and provide some resources such as: Cheerleading and encouragement Share information about resources Some state staff and/or consultant support At least partial funding of training/travel and VolunteerMatch for all or pilot group of libraries Sends letter with key volunteerism book to all library directors	State librarian willing to provide some level of support such as: Cheerleading and encouragement Share information about resources available through web links and newsletters.
Assign Project Leader(s) *NOTE: Key here is effort + time, not who specifically*	Project leader engaged with volunteers; spends time working with and coaching libraries *Start-up:* 40–50% time + consultant/trainer + some support staff time *Sustain:* 30%, or less + consultant and field volunteer(s)	Project leader engaged with volunteers; spends time working with and coaching libraries *Start-up:* 20–30% time, some support staff time *Sustain:* 10%, + consultant and/or field volunteer(s)	Project leader may be consultant or regional system leader who shares resources and information with libraries. *Start-up:* 5–10% time staff time *Sustain:* 2–3% + field volunteer(s)

Seek Input from Field	Analyze existing data Recruit task force of library staff champions and some volunteers to: • Review data • Identify key issues/potential barriers to implementation • Recommend additional research on key topics Consider all sizes of libraries. Share results with the field.	Analyze existing data Interview some library staff champions about key issues/barriers to implementation. Survey libraries regarding current volunteer practices. If available, use an existing task force to review results and make recommendations. Consider all sizes of libraries. Share results with the field.	Analyze existing data Interview some library staff champions. Consider all sizes of libraries. Share results with the field.
Pilot Test to Develop Success Stories	Identify a few library staff champions and get them started building results that can be shared. State library "Walks the Walk" engages volunteers and generates success stories for sharing.	Identify a few libraries already having success with skilled volunteers, and document those for sharing.	Use California, Texas, Arizona, and Idaho library success stories as examples.

(*continued*)

Get Involved: Powered by Your Library—Possible Scalable Approaches for Successful Replication by States (*continued*)

Success Factors	For Maximum Results	For Great Results	For Good Results
Training/Share Vision *NOTE: Three key training pieces required:* • *Vision—skilled volunteers become engaged advocates* • *Volunteer program implementation and infrastructure needs* • *Use of online tools*	Library application and selection process (exclusive access) Select applicant library teams (three to five people including top management) for two-day all-expense-paid training. Produce webinars—topics based on needs identified in surveys Periodic web-based "coaching" Facilitate cross-training between libraries and regional systems. Share webinars, online training, and other useful resources and promote www.getinvolvedclearinghouse.org	State library identifies library participants based on observation. Minimum two participants/library trained, including a manager—some travel expenses paid Archived and free live webinars and online training information shared with the field (including the Get Involved online clearinghouse—www.getinvolvedclearinghouse.org) Share information about CA's online course in volunteer engagement. Facilitate cross-training between libraries and regional systems.	Archived and free live webinars and online training information shared with the field (including the Get Involved online clearinghouse—www.getinvolvedclearinghouse.org) Share information about CA's online course in volunteer engagement.
VolunteerMatch (VM)	Purchase upgraded VM accounts for *all* libraries; access to VM libraries "hub" and VM support. Utilize VM training resources. Create a "widget" for library websites to increase hub results.	Purchase upgraded VM accounts for *selected* libraries; access to VM libraries "hub" and VM support. Utilize VM training resources. Create a "widget" for library websites to increase hub results	Make libraries aware of VM and potentially other online tools they can access for free or for a fee. Share availability of free training and other resources available from VM and www.getinvolvedclearinghouse.org

Communication, Marketing, and Promotion	Announces as a new campaign with a fancy rollout that articulates the mission Applications announced to attend training as exclusive opportunity State branding developed: posters, bookmarks, post cards, etc. Share results and success stories through a listserv for the project Workshops on the effort at state library association conferences and meetings Preconference on the effort at state library association conferences and meetings	Introductory e-mail to libraries from state librarian to articulate the mission of the effort (perhaps including a book on volunteer engagement) State branding developed Periodic updates to share results and success stories through an existing listserv Workshops on the effort at state library association conferences and meetings	Introductory e-mail to libraries to articulate the mission of the effort Periodic updates to share results and success stories through an existing listserv
Measure/Share Results *NOTE: Three key types of data will be collected:* • *Output—increase in volunteer hours/FTE* • *Output—number of volunteer opportunities posted on VM and number of volunteer connections made* • *Outcomes—survey volunteers registered on the hub for attitude and behavior changes*	Identify a statewide baseline of volunteer activity (annual statistics survey or other means) in order to track increases in outputs. Utilize VM statistics provided on number of library volunteer opportunities posted and number of connections made Survey volunteers from VM sign-ups for outcomes. Create and distribute nice visual annual reports on successes.	Identify a statewide baseline of volunteer activity (annual statistics survey or other means) in order to track increases in outputs. Consider only starting with libraries who are at least already tracking volunteer hours Utilize VM statistics provided on number of library volunteer opportunities posted and number of connections made.	No statewide baseline identified—just share success stories Local libraries maintain own stats Share ROI information developed by the volunteerism field. Share CA/VM Library Program Improvement Model to assist libraries in increasing their volunteer engagement capacity.

(*continued*)

Get Involved: Powered by Your Library—Possible Scalable Approaches for Successful Replication by States (*continued*)

Success Factors	For Maximum Results	For Great Results	For Good Results
	Utilize CA/VM Library Program Improvement Model as pretest/posttest of increased capacity (and to identify training needs) Share ROI information developed by the volunteerism field. Engage an external evaluator.	Survey volunteers from VM sign-ups for outcomes. Share ROI information developed by the volunteerism field. Utilize CA/VM Library Program Improvement Model as pre- and post-assessment of increased capacity (and to identify training needs).	
Sustainability/Ongoing Support to Participating Libraries	Use Idaho's MOU: identify what's expected (Years 1, 2, 3) (hours per month; number of opportunities posted on VM; use of widget, etc.). Listserv and webinars VolunteerMatch coaching calls State-developed web presence and online clearinghouse Regional leaders develop meetings for networking/problem Solving. Encourage use of Volunteer Program Improvement Model.	Use Idaho's MOU concept: to identify what's expected (Years 1, 2, 3) (hours per month; number of opportunities posted on VM; use of widget, etc.). Listserv Partner on "clearinghouse," webinars, and VM coaching calls. Identify experts in the field to assist as needed. Encourage use of Library Volunteer Program Improvement Model.	Share availability of free training and other resources available. Encourage use of Get Involved "clearinghouse" of resources. Listserv Encourage connections with local volunteer program coordinator networks. Encourage use of Library Volunteer Program Improvement Model.

Note: Final Version—rev. June 5, 2015.

Acknowledgments

The author wishes to thank Susan Hildreth, who championed this initiative from the beginning as State Librarian of California. Much appreciation goes also to her successors—Stacey Aldrich, Gerry Maginnity, and Greg Lucas, who felt strongly enough about the project's outcomes that they continued both staff and funding support for it. Thanks also to InfoPeople and the California State Library for permission to quote and adapt materials developed for the project.

Others who deserve thanks include:

My colleague at the California State Library Suzanne Flint, who masterminded the "Transforming Life After 50" project, from which the Get Involved initiative became a spinoff, and consultant Stephen Ristau, who used his considerable talents to assist with the implementation of both.

The intrepid California Get Involved "pilot" libraries who agreed to be trained early and implement skilled volunteer engagement practices in advance of rolling the initiative out to libraries throughout the state in order for us to be able to showcase early success stories—Marin County Library, Roseville Public Library, San Bernardino County Library, San Jose Public Library, St. Helena Public Library, and Torrance Public Library.

The late Jill Friedman Fixler and her associate Jennifer Rackow designed and delivered the initial training for California libraries.

A hardy group of library staff from throughout the state who stepped up to serve as Regional Leaders, to organize, lead, and recruit additional participants to Get Involved Regional Networks, allowing volunteer engagement leaders from libraries in their region to meet in person periodically to share ideas and problem solve.

The Institute for Museum and Library Services, who provided the funding for the Get Involved Planning Grant, and for the three-year grant to the four-state Get Involved Collaborative.

The state library members of the Get Involved Collaborative from each participating state—Donna Throckmorton in Arizona, Jennifer Peters in Texas, and Sue Walker in Idaho, and to their state librarians who approved their involvement with the project.

Paula MacKinnon of Califa, who together with her staff has deftly handled the event planning and administrative responsibilities for the grants.

Greg Baldwin, president of VolunteerMatch, who helped us see where this could go from the very beginning, and has supported and championed it within his national networks.

So many of the VolunteerMatch staff over the years have contributed immensely to the design of our partnership—Maura, Seth, Kevin, Jennifer, Samir—and Tessa, who agreed to review what I wrote about how VolunteerMatch works to be sure I got it right.

Barbara Ittner, whose editing guidance made this a better book.

And probably most of all, I want to thank the hundreds of library directors, staff, and volunteers who have embraced these concepts, inspired me with their success, and told me their stories so I could share them with you.

1

Why Volunteers?

Do you ever read or hear about exciting new library initiatives being implemented in other communities and think to yourself, "I wish we had the staff to make that happen?" If so, think again—maybe you can use volunteer talent to try appealing new ideas. Volunteers in today's libraries are doing everything from graphic design to event planning, public relations, grant writing, and more.

This book is meant to be a hands-on guide for libraries that wish to upgrade volunteer involvement to expand or enhance services, reach out to new customers, and gain advocates and supporters along the way. It will be useful to library directors, librarians, and other staff who wish to increase and build on their services to the community, and for library support groups who may need to revitalize volunteer engagement in their operations.

It's not just another book about library volunteers, but a guide to increasing your library's community engagement by cultivating volunteers who not only love the library and the work they do on its behalf, but are willing to be library ambassadors with their community connections and circles of influence.

The new library volunteerism is about more than getting materials back on the shelf, preparing for the annual book sale, or cleaning the gum off *Curious George*. What does your library need help with? What service would you like to add or expand to better meet the needs of your community? Do you need flyers designed? Displays arranged? A ukulele or yoga class? A job resource center? A maker program for teens? The possibilities are limitless. Imagine what you might accomplish if you had the right people willing and able to help you do it.

Assuming you do have some needs, let's start with why you might want to go down this new volunteer engagement path. What are the benefits of engaging volunteers?

BENEFITS OF ENGAGING VOLUNTEERS AT THE LIBRARY

Benefit 1: Volunteers Help to Enhance or Expand Library Services

Libraries can broaden services in response to community needs by deploying volunteers to deliver materials to the homebound, after-school "homework help" programs, adult literacy tutoring, and one-to-one or classroom computer instruction. Engaging skilled volunteers enables the library to add or expand these services beyond what could be accomplished with limited staff time.

Volunteers can also enhance current services because they have the time to provide one-on-one support. Although a staff member may love a chance to take the time to help someone for an hour, the demands of the job usually make that impossible. A volunteer, however, has the luxury of time, and could provide that level of support needed to help someone solve a problem or learn something new.

Benefit 2: Volunteers Bring Specialized Skills

Most libraries offer "traditional" volunteer jobs like book shelver, book mender, and "Friend." But for many of today's volunteers, those positions have limited appeal. Although it is possible of course to find those who will gladly shelve or mend books, many potential volunteers have a host of other impressive skills and are willing to share them.

When a need arises that you don't have the skills for or available staff, consider designing a volunteer role. If you need a public relations specialist, graphic designer, photographer, job coach, or merchandising expert for the book sale, there are people in your community who have those skills who would be willing to volunteer their time if they understood the need, and how they might be able to help.

Benefit 3: Volunteers Share Their Connections

Volunteers have full lives outside the library. You might think of them as the "tutor" or "homebound delivery volunteer," without considering the fact that they have a full life beyond this role. They have relationships with other organizations, might go to a church, be a member of a civic club, or work for a business or corporation that has resources that could be made available to the library.

Many of the corporations and businesses where volunteers (or their family and friends) work, provide resources for employees to help and encourage their community service—often in-kind donations like access to in-house printing services, gifts of used office equipment, matching a volunteer's financial contribution to the organization they volunteer for, or even providing "release time" that allows volunteering during work hours.

Volunteers also can connect you to a segment of your service population you want to reach out to—a minority community, age group, or geographic area. Ask volunteers to help build relationships across perceived ethnic, age, or geographic barriers.

When thinking about how to broaden the library's community connections, a meaningful place to start is with your volunteers. But remember, they can't bring you resources and connections if they don't know you're looking for them.

Benefit 4: Volunteers Supplement Staff Time

One of any library's most precious commodities is the time of its library staff. Save some of that professional staff time by giving volunteers the jobs to do that staff don't have the skills or time to complete. This will free up some professional librarian time to attend to the highly skilled tasks they were trained to do.

Benefit 5: Volunteers Bring New Energy and Ideas

This is what keeps me in the volunteer business. Volunteers propose approaches that I would never have thought about. They can spark a new idea, bring a different perspective, or suggest a creative approach. They reenergize me. It's always great to see the library through the fresh eyes of a volunteer who understands the important work of the library and wants to be involved in it.

Benefit 6: Engaged Volunteers Naturally Transform into Strong Library Supporters

This benefit lies at the heart of this book. Once people understand the library's issues and are able to see and care about its role in the community, they begin to feel a part of the library's "tribe" and will gladly share their skills and resources to support it, be its advocate during the budget process, and promote its worth with the community.

This isn't just about getting the work done, or even just about bringing new skills to the library, although of course both of those are important. This is about using volunteer engagement as a strategy to engage people more with the library. It's about reaching out and building a community of library supporters who we often didn't even know before and who maybe hadn't been in the library for a very long time.

Decision makers often view volunteers as more credible spokespersons for the library than staff or even the library's director. This is because when staff advocate for the library to the city council, the county board of supervisors or other funders can be perceived as self-interested—trying to save their jobs. When volunteers talk to decision makers—or go with you—the library's request is now being made by community members and constituents. Volunteers make terrific messengers.

When a library begins a push to raise funds, such as developing a foundation or a bond measure, critical to that effort will be the breadth and depth of community support for it. Key to that effort will be a committed and diverse group of volunteers.

In a 2017 article, Erin Rebecca Spink[1] suggests: "One of the most undervalued assets volunteers can bring to your organization is an enhancement of your organizational reputation . . . take a moment to consider what difference it could make to your organization if every one of the volunteers connected to you acted as a positive ambassador, singing your praises publicly to their networks . . ."

Benefit 7: Volunteers Give More

The 2016 edition of "Volunteering and Civic Life in America"[2] demonstrated not for the first time that volunteerism has a direct relationship to financial contributions. The study found that 79 percent of volunteers donated to charity, while only 40 percent of nonvolunteers did.

The opportunity to raise more money, however, should never be the primary goal of a volunteer engagement effort. Although the potential for increased fund-raising can be a secondary outcome, it should never be the primary reason to engage volunteers in the library's work.

WHAT WILL GET IN YOUR WAY? UNION ISSUES AND STAFF RESISTANCE

This may seem an odd heading in a chapter on *why* you might want to utilize volunteers, but in working on this issue for some years, it's become clear that although you may be getting excited about the idea, you've also begun to think about *why not*, so it's best to address the two key concerns up front, in order to not distract you from the exciting possibilities presented by engaging volunteers in libraries.

The biggest potential barriers to implementing volunteer engagement will probably be internal. If your library's workers are unionized, pushback could begin there—not necessarily from the union itself, but from staff, managers, and even the library director, who may believe that the collective bargaining agreement limits the use of volunteers.

This issue arose early in the development of California's "Get Involved" initiative, so we interviewed library directors from a variety of libraries and found that their collective bargaining agreements had no specific language on using volunteers. Most, however, said that they had at least an "unwritten agreement" with the union that volunteers would not supplant employees.

These library leaders strongly suggested that each library review its union contract, engage union leadership early in the planning process for development or expansion of volunteer engagement, and develop a mission statement clarifying that the role of volunteers is to supplement, and not to supplant, the work of paid staff.

Even if your library doesn't have unionized workers, it is not uncommon to experience some staff resistance to expanding volunteer engagement. Staff concerns usually come from fear of their jobs being replaced by volunteers or about decreased service quality. They may also resent a perceived additional workload being thrust on them—taking on volunteer management responsibilities. You can watch 30-minute video of an interview with two library directors about how they dealt with both the union issue and staff resistance.[3]

Some staff have had a previous bad experience working with volunteers. Although much of that can likely be blamed on poor volunteer recruitment, training, or management practices, those experiences make those staff less likely to jump on the volunteer engagement bandwagon.

There are a number of strategies that can be employed to gain staff buy-in for volunteer engagement that are discussed in Chapter 5, "Success Factors for Volunteer Engagement," but one key strategy that can and should be addressed up front is to develop a mission statement for volunteer engagement at your library.

DEVELOPING A VOLUNTEER ENGAGEMENT MISSION STATEMENT

Most libraries have a mission statement that lays out broad purposes and outlines goals for its service to the community. A similar statement is needed for volunteer engagement efforts.

The California State Library's (CSL) volunteer policy and procedures manual can be used as an example.[4] Note that it shows a commitment to staff, and at the same time states the value of volunteers and the organization's intent to utilize them for important purposes.

"Volunteers are unpaid individuals who dedicate time and talent to support programs and projects of the CSL. Volunteers are offered an opportunity to share their skills, gain new skills, and meet new people, and are considered a valuable resource.

The purposes of the Volunteer Engagement Program are to:

- Support and/or supplement, *but not supplant* the assignments of employees and special projects;
- Enrich the CSL's programs with special interest and skills of volunteers; and
- Promote community awareness of the CSL and its services.

The objectives of the Volunteer Engagement Program are to:

- Provide volunteers the opportunity to contribute their skills and time to projects that support the mission and goals of the CSL;
- Develop volunteer assignments to extend the resources of the CSL; and
- Develop public awareness of the roles and resources of the CSL."

When developing your own volunteer engagement mission statement, don't sit alone in your office and just write your version. Involve other key players—your director, plus key staff and volunteers, including the Friends and the board, and a union representative if applicable.

The best approach is to constitute a volunteer engagement team made up of these key players. Guidance from all the interested parties from the very beginning will help to overcome resistance because you now have "allies" throughout the organization who have contributed and therefore feel some ownership of volunteer engagement.

It's very important that before beginning, your volunteer engagement team checks to see if your library's governing jurisdiction has an existing volunteer mission statement designed to be used by all departments. If so, be sure you understand its intent, communicate it to staff and volunteers, and implement it as stated.

If you do write your own mission statement, it should be approved based on your library's governing body.

Here are some steps you can follow to create your own volunteer engagement mission statement:

1. Give the volunteer engagement team a homework assignment. Ask them to review some sample mission statements and then write four statements to finish this phrase:

   The _______________ Library connects community members with information that supports lifelong learning in a welcoming atmosphere with knowledgeable staff, and believes that engaging volunteers will assist in achieving this. As a result, we believe the following related to volunteer engagement at the library:

Tell them not to be limited to what they see in the sample mission statements (see samples and homework assignment in the Appendices for this chapter). Give them a couple weeks to do the assignment and return it to you. If you prefer to gather such sample mission statements from sources near you, that's fine too.

2. Compile the statements that are returned to you without passing judgment. Include all statements that were submitted, without editing. This allows all who participated to see their ideas in writing and really feel part of the process, even if ultimately their statement doesn't get included or isn't exactly as they wrote it. Group them according to common themes that emerge: volunteers as a link to the community; volunteers' relationship to staff; expand/enhance services with volunteers, etc. Use whatever themes jump out at you.
3. At the next scheduled meeting of your volunteer engagement team, review the compilation of everyone's statements. With all the statements in front of them, people can easily begin to see where there is agreement, and consensus can be reached quickly in those areas. You can facilitate a discussion of all the statements within the full group, or break them into smaller groups to work on each "theme" and report their recommendations back to the full group.
4. When consensus is reached, circulate a draft statement for comment after the meeting. A second draft is then circulated for fine-tuning. Have a vote or approval process by the team once it's complete, so it's clear that it has been formally accepted. Then, have it approved by the library director and board, so they understand and gain ownership of it as well.

   If consensus is not reached on one or more themes or statements, there's more work to do, with the full group, or in small groups assigned a specific task. Ask a couple of other libraries about their statements on a particular issue; then share those results as potential verbiage for the team's review and revision.

When you use such a process to develop your mission statement, it helps to avoid the two biggest barriers to your success—union pushback and staff resistance. The agreed-on statement is then used to decide what direction to take when issues or problems arise. Approval by the governing body means they have been educated about these issues and will support it into the future as a formally approved policy.

GET A VOLUNTEER TO DO IT: MYTHS ABOUT VOLUNTEERS

Volunteerism sometimes gets a bad rap because of some commonly held myths. These myths are often perpetuated by policy-making bodies or funders, who assume that regardless of the situation, every problem can be solved by finding a volunteer to handle it.

In the following paragraphs, these myths are debunked in order that you have a response when they come up, that you don't get discouraged when they do, and that you feel empowered to get on with the important work of accomplishing amazing things by engaging volunteers.

Myth 1: Volunteers Can Replace Paid Staff

Let's face it—99.9 percent of volunteers do not come to you with advanced degrees in library science. But they can assist librarians. When volunteers handle tasks that aren't "library technical," it frees up some librarian hours for them to complete their professional duties.

Local elected officials often don't understand the highly technical aspects of library work, which leads them to suggest that you just "get a volunteer to do it." They don't do this because they're hateful or dumb; they do it because they don't understand what a professional librarian does. It's on you, librarians, to help them understand. Show them the technical aspects of librarianship—they'll be amazed and impressed. And volunteer engagement won't be the only situation where their knowledge of what a professional librarian does can be both relevant and useful.

Provide tours of the library. Show them what goes on behind the scenes. Bring them in when the computer lab is filled to the brim with students, job seekers, and seniors. Introduce them to your maker space, and to your collections in Spanish and Tagalog.

Please don't wait for a budget cut proposal to bring these decision makers on board. Build a strong relationship and understanding of library services, needs, and goals on an ongoing basis.

Myth 2: Volunteers Are Free

"Because volunteers are often regarded as 'free,' the notion that they might require an investment seems paradoxical. As one executive director noted in our focus group, '*Volunteering sounds like it's free and not worth anything*,' thus, '. . . *it's tough to convince the board to use money for volunteers*.' Although it's true that volunteers operate without receiving market-value compensation for the work performed, serious organizational initiatives—of any type—require a strategic vision and an outlay of time, attention, and infrastructure"[5] (Rehnborg, 2015).

Some staff time must be applied to the process of volunteer engagement in order to get the results we're talking about. A few resources are also needed to train volunteers, provide a workspace, and keep track of and thank them for their efforts.

Volunteer engagement can help to expand services and increase productivity, but be clear with policy makers and the library director—it can certainly be cost effective and can dramatically expand community engagement, but it's not free.

Myth 3: Volunteers Are Self-Managing

Volunteers bring good intentions and wonderful skills, but they don't know how the library works or where they fit in. In addition to orientation about the library, and training or guidance for the job they've accepted, volunteers expect that their time will be used wisely and not be wasted. Some planning, organization, and management skills will need to be applied.

If volunteers have a bad experience because these issues haven't been addressed, your efforts at community engagement can be stymied quickly. The goal must be to engage volunteers in a productive way—and not just for the library, but meaningfully for the volunteer as well. Some staff time will need to be assigned to organizing the volunteer engagement efforts effectively.

CHAPTER SUMMARY

You've hopefully concluded from this chapter that engaging skilled volunteers is an important strategy for libraries—to enhance and expand services, to attract new community members to the library, and to watch them naturally become library advocates and supporters. You've seen that these goals have successfully been achieved through a statewide initiative in California, and that major barriers to implementation can be overcome.

But if you need further convincing, consider these words from our colleague, Cathy Crosthwaite, acting community engagement manager, Sacramento Public Library.[6]

"The Great Recession brought a need into libraries that hadn't been seen for many years. Entrenched views about volunteers in the library needed to be addressed in order to accommodate the growing number of people that wanted to give back.

The skills that come with these people are noteworthy and have the ability to enhance the library's efforts in certain areas that staff could never have accommodated. This holds true for volunteers that fill positions as adult literacy tutors, job coaches, computer coaches, book sale coordinators, grant writers, etc.

We are able to offer crafting classes with advanced knitters, quilters, painters, or hold writing workshops with retired English teachers or creative writing professors. Teens are included in this scenario as they volunteer to organize teen-centric programming or do one-on-one computer help for seniors. Volunteers are able to fill these roles that satisfy a community need without taking up significant library resources.

Volunteers now assist with outreach efforts, coordinate our annual Teen Yule Ball, assist veterans with their questions and concerns, help people find jobs, and work with school-age students on their homework questions. These services were previously not available to the community.

When someone has experienced excellent customer service, or better yet, has taken part in or helped to improve that service, he or she will tell people about it and encourage people to support that institution. Volunteers will not take our jobs. There is just too much to do for that to ever happen. But volunteers can make it possible for library staff to fill the needs in our communities in ways previously thought unattainable."

Now sit back and enjoy the specifics and hands-on tools contained in the following chapters. You'll learn what's new in volunteer engagement, how to implement new strategies, and the factors that will ensure your success.

NOTES

1. Spink, Erin Rebecca, "Volunteers Are the Reputational Assets Your Organization Is Overlooking." https://www.linkedin.com/pulse/volunteers-reputational-assets-your-organization-spink-ma (accessed October 19, 2017).

2. Corporation for National & Community Service, "Volunteering and Civic Life in America," 2016. https://www.nationalservice.gov/vcla/national (accessed January 18, 2017).

3. Early in the Get Involved initiative it was determined that the two biggest potential internal barriers to moving toward engagement of skilled volunteers in your library would be union issues and staff resistance. This 30-minute video is an interview with two library directors about how they handled each of those issues. Go to https://getinvolvedclearinghouse.org/resource/training-materials/library-directors-discuss-union-issues-and-staff-buy (accessed February 13, 2018).

4. http://getinvolvedca.org/resource/management-tools/volunteer-policies-and-procedures-california-state-library (accessed October 18, 2017).

5. Rosenthal, Robert J., Ed., *Volunteer Engagement 2.0: Ideas and Insights Changing the World* (Hoboken, NJ: Wiley & Sons, 2015), p. 37.

6. Comments by Cathy Crosthwaite, acting community engagement manager, Sacramento (CA) Public Library (via e-mail January 2017).

Sample Library Volunteer Engagement Mission Statements

I. City Library: Volunteer Program Mission Statement

The library's mission is to inform, to enhance the quality of life, and to foster lifelong learning. The library is committed to the idea that involving volunteers in its operation will assist it in carrying out its mission for the community. Therefore, we believe that:

- Volunteers allow the library to provide enhanced services to the community.
- Volunteers provide a vital link between the library and the community—both by informing the community about the services the library has to offer and by bringing valuable community input to the library planning process.
- A thoughtfully planned and well-managed volunteer program can bring a wealth of benefits to the library, its staff, the community, and the volunteers.
- A successful volunteer program requires that staff and volunteers work as a team to implement the mission and goals of the library.
- Volunteers supplement, but do not supplant, library staff; volunteers complement, but do not replace, library staff.

II. County Library: Volunteer Program Mission Statement

The county library believes that involving volunteers in its operation will assist in carrying out its vision. Volunteers serve as an important link between the library and the community. They help the community to understand how the library works, as well as its importance as a community cultural, educational, and recreation resource. And, by bringing in the consumer viewpoint, volunteers expand library personnel's understanding of community needs and interests.

Library service is enhanced by volunteers supplementing and assisting the library staff. Volunteers bring ability, talent, and time, allowing staff to provide enhanced services and embark on special projects. Volunteers are welcome to help in all facets of the library operation except in functions that would jeopardize patron confidentiality and their right to privacy.

III. City Administrative Policy and Procedure on Volunteerism

PURPOSE: This administrative policy is established to set forth in writing the city's intent to encourage the continuation and expansion of its use of volunteers as a valuable human resource, as well as an opportunity to fully involve the community in city government.

OBJECTIVE: The city values its many volunteers, and relies on them to provide support and assistance in areas where permanent city staffing is unavailable, not feasible, or augmentation would assist current staff or enhance services. Volunteers support regular staff and existing programs but do not take the lead in developing and implementing ongoing programs and services currently performed by city staff.

The use of volunteers is encouraged. However, they may not be used to replace or supplant city employees. In a layoff or freeze situation, the city will not support continuation of current service levels through use of volunteer support. If a program or staff position is offered as a program cut, the department may not plan to fill the vacancy with volunteers.

IV. County Volunteer Program Philosophy

Volunteers are those who give their skills without pay to an organization. County volunteers will complement, not replace, paid staff positions. County volunteers are to be treated as members of the team of people providing service to the citizenry of the county. Thoughtful planning and implementation of a volunteer program will bring rich benefits to the county, its paid employees, its citizens, and the volunteers themselves.

Mission Statement Homework Assignment

LIBRARY VOLUNTEER ENGAGEMENT TEAM

Date Due: ________

Purpose of the Assignment: Job one in the development or expansion of volunteer engagement is to "set the tone" for the program in a mission statement. The mission answers basic philosophical questions against which all program plans are measured, like *why* volunteers are utilized, *how* they fit into the organizational structure, and *how* they will be treated.

Step 1: Review the above Sample Mission Statements—these are from actual libraries (or the city or county to which they are accountable). These samples should give you some ideas, *but don't be limited by them.* You'll find as you review them that each one sets a different tone—it gives you a real feel for how that entity approaches the concept of volunteerism, and how much it values it. As you read you'll begin to see the kinds of important policy questions they answer, which can be helpful when planning decisions must be made.

The idea behind a mission statement is that it's *ours*—it should reflect our library's approach, philosophy, and tone. Each of you should think about what you hope for in terms of volunteer engagement—what you think is important about it, what goals and standards it should achieve, etc. So, use the samples only to spark ideas—none of them are right or wrong, they're just *theirs.*

Step 2: Write four statements or phrases below, to finish this:

> The ______________ Library connects community members with information that supports lifelong learning in a welcoming atmosphere with knowledgeable staff, and believes that engaging volunteers will assist in achieving this. As a result, we believe the following related to volunteer engagement at the library:

1.
2.
3.
4.

Step 3: Be sure I receive your four statements by this date _______ and I will compile our collective thoughts for our meeting on this date ________:

*Name, Address, Phone, FAX, E-mail here**

*Although you may have an internal sharing drive or consider using DropBox, GoogleDrive, or other similar technology, one of the old-fashioned ways of getting the information to you might be better in this case because you will be the only one who knows which statements were submitted by which team member. For example, you want to avoid any embarrassment by keeping each submission confidential, and you don't want the library director's statements to hold more sway than those of other team members if they can see them in advance.

2

Volunteerism Trends Changing the Landscape

Consider volunteer engagement as one strategy for getting more members of your community involved with the library. An added benefit to this approach is that successfully engaged volunteers can very naturally transform into library supporters and advocates. This chapter looks at what you need to know about volunteerism trends and changing demographics in order to reap those benefits.

CONSIDER THESE TRENDS

Trend 1: Generational Differences

> **Generation:** A group of individuals born and living contemporaneously who have common knowledge and experiences that affect their thoughts, attitudes, values, beliefs, and behaviors.[1]

During the mid-2000s, as baby boomers began to turn 50, research revealed that no longer would traditional volunteer roles be enough to attract this generation of volunteers.[2–4] Boomers were interested in volunteer opportunities that would use their skills, allow flexibility, use their time wisely, and demonstrate how their efforts would make a difference.

More recently, similar observations have been made about younger generations' interests in volunteerism. "Licking envelopes won't cut it. Millennials demand more out of their volunteer experiences. 75% of Millennials think their biggest impact comes from contributions other than financial, such as skills-based volunteering . . ."[5]

Although the California State Library's Get Involved initiative focused initially on baby-boomer volunteers, libraries quickly learned that much of the retooling of their volunteer engagement practices to attract boomers also helps with outreach to the generations that follow.

Before we get started, let's put in context this look at generational differences. Although an individual's worldview is partially shaped by issues and events that occur during his or her formative years, the discussion of generations below are generalizations and won't fit every single boomer, gen Xer, or millennial. They can be a good rule of thumb to help understand what each group's volunteerism interests and issues might be, but they are certainly not absolutes that define your encounters with every single member of a particular generation.

The Silent Generation (Born 1926–1945)

The silent generation are basically your current senior volunteers. They came of age around World War II and are guided by their values of patriotism, belief in the power of institutions, respect for authority, and selflessness. Their path to volunteerism came from a sense of obligation, and therefore they are often willing to do whatever is needed in order to help. Many women were not in the workforce, and volunteering allowed socializing as well as service. Sean Connery and Judi Dench are part of the silent generation.

Baby Boomers (Born 1946–1964)

Boomers came of age during the Vietnam War and Watergate—human, environmental, women's, and civil rights also experienced important gains during that time. They are the generation that the Peace Corps was founded for and JFK challenged to think about what they could do for their country. Because many see themselves as activists, they expect volunteer opportunities that inspire them. Because most have been in the workforce, they want the opportunity to put their skills to use. And because consumerism has exploded during their lifetime, they expect an abundance of volunteer options to choose from.

Boomers are "willing to volunteer, but they want flexibility, work that taps into their skills and evidence that they've made a difference—not things previous volunteers needed . . . unlike the generation before them, boomers don't want to be chained to a schedule or tied to one organization. They want the freedom to jump from cause to cause or take months off to travel."[6]

California's research showed that most libraries think they are prepared to engage boomer volunteers because they've been so successful over the years with senior volunteers. Here's the catch—boomers are not the "senior" volunteers you're used to working with. Oprah Winfrey and George Clooney are baby boomers.

Most boomers view aging very differently from their parents, and above all, don't want to be called "seniors," "retirees," "elderly," or "older adults!" It's for this reason that you've seen many organizations change their names—AARP, for example, is no longer the American Association of Retired People—it's just AARP. And Elder Hostel changed its name to "Road Scholar" for their incoming audience. Reaching out to the boomers by asking for "senior volunteers" will most likely cause them to run in the opposite direction.

Generation X (Born 1965–1980)

Gen Xers were the latchkey generation as many women found their way into the workforce, so they are often independent and self-reliant. They were the first generation to experience personal computers, cable TV, and video games in their young lives. They like informality and fun but are very focused on their career paths, and feel they've been held back because the baby boomers won't retire. Engaging gen Xers as volunteers will mean your technology must be up to date—everything online and current. They will be looking for flexible options and exposure to opportunities that could help to advance their careers. Christina Aguilera and Matt Damon are gen Xers.

The Corporation for National and Community Service found in its 2015 Volunteering and Civic Life in America research[7] that 28.9 percent of generation X volunteers are volunteering primarily in education and youth service activities, probably because as of this writing, they are ages 37–54, and many have children at home. Even though their current rate of volunteering is higher than the other generations (boomers, 25.7 percent, millennials, 21.9 percent), not as much research has been done on gen X volunteering—most likely because the gen X cohort at approximately 50 million is comparably smaller than either the boomers (76 million) or the millennials (80 million).

Millennials (Born 1981–2002)

Millennials are digital natives, born into a high tech society, and the first generation to embrace online networking. They came of age around the Gulf War and the September 11 attack. Their values include life-long learning and achieving a work-life balance. They reject prejudice and are wired for collaboration and working in groups. They learned community organizing through social media. Ryan Gosling and Justin Bieber are millennials.

The Millennial Impact Project[8] is a comprehensive and trusted study of the millennial generation and their involvement with causes. Consider this from their five-year trend retrospective[9]: "When we began our research, this generation was most often described in negative terms: Lazy. Apathetic. Entitled. Five years later, we have amassed data that inarguably refutes those notions. As a result, we have reached one overarching conclusion: The size and force of the millennial generation combined with social media and pivotal world events of the past five years require nonprofits to develop new ways of engaging audiences lest they risk being left behind as millennial preferences fundamentally alter cause engagement.

In analyzing five years of research data, we identified six common findings:

1. Intrinsic passion for a cause is millennials' primary motivator.
2. Millennials volunteer and give modestly to multiple causes in early engagement.
3. Among millennials, women give more money than men, and older individuals more than younger ones; larger donations correlate with higher total volunteer hours.
4. Peers are a critical influence on millennial giving.
5. Millennials want to use and develop their skills through cause engagement.
6. Millennials learn about and donate to causes digitally, using each platform distinctly."

The report concludes that millennials' engagement in causes reflects their desire to do good, and that their engagement will expand as they age and as community organizations learn to connect with them more effectively. The research reflects the strong potential for engaging this group.

A June 2017 Pew Research report[10] showed that millennials are the most likely generation of Americans to use public libraries, which makes it even more important that we strive to engage them as volunteers.

Again, the goal of reviewing this generational information is not to "pigeon-hole" people based on age but simply to be aware of potential differences in approaches to volunteers of different generations. Thinking of each generation as a monolith, with everyone in the group thinking or acting the same way, will not be productive.

A Special Word for Friends of the Library about Generational Issues

This discussion of generations is relevant to everyone in library land, but because many libraries' Friends are aging out of their positions, and many are not having success bringing in younger volunteers to sustain their work, this information might be of particular interest. Proceeds from Friends' book sales and other activities are major contributors to library book budgets and special programming across the country, so not paying attention to this issue could not only be sad, but costly! If your Friends are still holding their meetings in the middle of the workday, have not expanded their volunteer opportunities beyond boxing and sorting donated books, and are not considering how to reach out to gen X and millennial volunteers, their days as a viable organization may be numbered.

Trend 2: Skilled Volunteers

If the library's aim in engaging volunteers is to add or enhance a service, or complete a task that must be done by someone with a particular set of skills that are not available on your staff, you must reach out beyond the usual people and usual ways that volunteers have been found before, and attract new volunteers who have the skills that you need.

Imagine your Friends group had a volunteer skilled in merchandising to help with the book sale or your bookstore—how about an experienced store manager . . . a bookkeeper? Feel free to fantasize about a grant writer, a banker, a CPA, or an attorney to help your Library Foundation get off the ground . . . hopefully, you're beginning to see the possibilities!

REAL-LIFE EXAMPLE: SKILLED VOLUNTEERS

When it came time for the 30th anniversary celebration of California's statewide library literacy service, my statewide literacy coordinator team needed a seasoned public relations professional with experience planning regional or statewide campaigns to help achieve our goals of raising awareness about literacy and recruiting volunteer tutors. With a carefully designed public relations specialist volunteer job description, we found some candidates on LinkedIn.

During the interview process, one candidate stood out. His résumé showed the requisite experience, but it was what he shared in the interview that caught our attention. He said, "If it's OK with you, I'd like to share a plan I've started developing." He had been to our website, gained a very accurate view of what we were trying to accomplish, and had already begun designing a plan to accomplish it! Before the interview concluded, he said he wanted to tell us why he was so enthusiastic about getting this volunteer position. First, he said, it was because he had the experience we were looking for and was willing to share it for what he saw as an important cause. Additionally, he had just moved to the area to start his own PR firm, and although he had clients, he wasn't busy full time. He saw our volunteer position as a way to use some of his free time and gain some local experience, contacts, and references.[11]

People with the specialized skills you are looking for are often happy to share them as volunteers. In a recent LinkedIn survey, "82% of LinkedIn members said they wanted to volunteer their skills" (Garlinghouse and Dorsey, 2015).[12]

Sometimes use of the term "high-skilled" volunteer makes people think only of volunteers with a professional degree, but we certainly don't draw the line there. Volunteers with skills we need might have a college degree, but might not. We're talking about all kinds of skills that might be needed—from public relations experts and graphic designers to carpenters, artists, and experienced knitters or seamstresses.

Unfortunately, volunteer engagement leaders often limit themselves, as well as service to their community, by limiting consideration of services for the community to what they already know how to do, and by only reaching out to people that they already know. More success comes from not limiting yourself to who and what *you* already know, and instead, identifying high-impact volunteer positions, and then reaching out to people with the skills that can help to implement your ideas.

Trend 3: Shift from Volunteer Management to Volunteer Engagement

In the old days, libraries offered only entry-level volunteer jobs that any "warm body" could do. Many volunteer assignments were also offered because they were things that staff didn't want to do. Recruitment consisted of saying, "Come and be a library volunteer—just come in on Tuesdays and Thursdays from 10:00 to noon and we'll find something for you to do." One day they might be asked to cut the bunny ears for story time, and another day straighten the magazines or dust the shelves.

If you still have need for shift workers like these, you may be able to find some adults, teens, or court-appointed volunteers who are willing to do them, but that approach is really old school "volunteer management." Using today's approach—"volunteer engagement"—you'll be defining specific, meaningful jobs that need to be done to advance the library's mission, identifying the skills required to get them done well, and focusing your recruitment on finding volunteers with the specific skills to make it all happen.

Joan Young, former volunteer coordinator for the San Jose Public Library (SJPL), describes their need to transition from volunteer management to engagement: "Our library's volunteer management program was outdated. . . . Under the traditional volunteer management model, nearly anyone interested in volunteering was accepted. Volunteers were given specific tasks to complete, many of them clerical, and told exactly how the task should be accomplished. Further, volunteers were expected to commit to ongoing service. A 'good' volunteer was defined by the number of years they volunteered."[13]

The example used to describe San Jose's transition to the volunteer engagement model is their expansion of volunteer-facilitated ESL Conversation Clubs to multiple branches. Instead of just seeking volunteers to facilitate the groups, they began by recruiting three volunteers with specific skills to serve as program coordinators. Skills for the coordinator positions included experience in the English language learning field, as well as project management, teamwork, and leadership skills. This team developed training for volunteers and then recruited, interviewed, and trained the new facilitators.

With this example in mind, let's take a look at the differences between volunteer *management* (where we've been) and volunteer *engagement* (where we're going) in Table 2.1.[14]

TABLE 2.1. From Volunteer Management to Engagement

Recruitment Recruitment primarily done through flyers, newsletters, and signs in the library for low-level positions that just about anyone can fill.	**Cultivation** Multiple targeted recruitment methods including staff and volunteer connections and collaborations with other organizations to identify potential volunteers who are selected based on the interests and skills required for specific high-impact volunteer roles.
Placement A narrow list of usually low-level positions to be completed at the library, on a set schedule, under staff supervision are offered. Each volunteer selects one of the roles and a scheduled shift for completing work.	**Selection/Negotiation/Agreement** Multiple volunteer assignments are developed for a wide range of skills and interests not limited to clerical and administrative positions. Volunteers are selected for their position based on their skills and interests. Staff and volunteers collaboratively negotiate project outcomes and timeline. Scheduling is flexible, and work may be done outside the office, even virtually.
Supervision Volunteer activity is directly supervised by staff. Usually no end date of service is determined.	**Feedback, Collaboration, and Support** Staff and skilled volunteers are colleagues. Often the volunteers are the subject matter experts, and they are provided support and guidance by staff on organizational policy, resources available, etc. Timeline includes an end date that can be renegotiated if necessary.
Evaluation/Review Volunteers do what they are assigned to do and may receive feedback. Contribution is often measured by hours or years of service.	**Measurement** Predetermined outcomes are measured to make an assessment of the impact of the volunteers' efforts on the organization's stated goals.

(*continued*)

TABLE 2.1. From Volunteer Management to Engagement (*continued*)

Recognition Volunteers are thanked usually through an annual event, and/or with pins, certificates, mugs, pens, or other items. Level of recognition is often based on length of service. Recognition is generally a one-size-fits-all approach.	**Acknowledgment** Acknowledgment includes sharing with the volunteers the impact their work has made on stated goals. Additional rewards are derived from the volunteers' interests, such as opportunities to learn or try something new, be exposed to a new approach or technique, or to get a chance to work with someone they admire and respect. Acknowledgement is determined based on what is meaningful to the volunteers. It's not a one-size-fits-all approach.
Retention Goal is to keep the volunteer in the position as long as possible. The volunteer is either asked to make a long commitment, or no definite time frame is discussed or agreed upon.	**Sustainability** Focus is on sustaining the work a volunteer does, not necessarily on keeping a volunteer forever. Strategies such as volunteer job sharing, cross-training, and team approaches are utilized so that the work continues when a volunteer leaves.

Trend 4: Corporate Volunteerism

You probably already know that many corporations support employee volunteer programs, but do you know why? Some do it primarily for the public relations value—but many also encourage volunteerism to build employee loyalty, job satisfaction, and teamwork within the organization.

"Fifty-two percent of U.S. employees are disengaged, meaning they fail to work at their full potential. . . . To regain employee attention and inspiration, some firms are looking to volunteerism as an employee engagement and team-building strategy . . ." (Johnson, 2015).[15]

In recent years, corporate social responsibility (CSR) policies have been introduced in many organizations. As defined by the University of Washington's Center for Leadership and Social Responsibility, "CSR is a process with the aim to embrace responsibility for the company's actions and encourage a positive impact through its activities on the environment, consumers, employees, communities, stakeholders and all other members of the public sphere who may also be considered as stakeholders."[16]

Corporate social responsibility policies often include the commitment to integrity and ethical business practices, protecting the environment, and serving the communities where they do business through philanthropy and volunteerism. Beyond just encouraging employees to volunteer, some companies also provide paid release time for employees to do so, financial donations to organizations that employees volunteer with, and/or organize one-day group volunteer projects with local organizations for employees to participate in.

In a 2017 *Wall Street Journal* article,[17] the author describes growing interest in corporate volunteering or "pro bono" work. Pro bono describes the opportunity for workers to donate their professional expertise. The rise in pro bono work hours (more than 1 million hours in 2016, more than 492,305 hours in 2013) "coincides with growth in the number of employers sponsoring pro-bono service programs. Many companies see these initiatives as a way to attract and retain professionals who desire more purposeful careers."

Also impacting the recent dramatic expansion of corporate social responsibility programs is that millennials value volunteering. In a 2016 article, "Why Company Sponsored Volunteer Programs Are Keeping Millennials at Work," *Forbes* explains: "Millennials today view work as an integrated part of their life, not a separate activity, so they are deeply concerned with ensuring that their company's values align with their own. . . . Young talent is unlikely to stick around an organization that operates contrary to their personal values. Further, companies that support an employee's efforts to advance causes they care about through volunteering programs stand to retain their talent. . . . 'Today, employees expect their companies to be good corporate citizens. . . . It's not a nice to do, it's a business imperative.'"[18]

The goal of business is to make a profit for their shareholders, but it's become increasingly clear that doing well can be enhanced by doing good.

What steps can you take to reap the benefits of corporate volunteerism for your library? First, if there's a company operating in your town—even if it's just a branch location—take the time to locate and read the statement of such policies on the company's website to get a sense of how you might participate. Check with staff, board, friends, and volunteers who may work there or have friends or family who do, to see what else you can learn about finding your way in.

Although there will be more about online recruitment strategies later in this chapter (see "Trend 5: Technology Advances") and later in Chapter 4, "Volunteer Recruitment," you should be aware that VolunteerMatch has partnerships with more than 100 companies with a total of 2.6 million employees. When a potential corporate volunteer searches for a volunteer opportunity in your zip code, he or she will be shown volunteer positions you have posted on VolunteerMatch.org via a web-based solution the company uses built by VolunteerMatch.

VolunteerMatch also partners with several corporate-giving platforms, such as Bright Funds, Causecast, and YourCause, to potentially bring your volunteer opportunities in front of millions more potential corporate volunteers. Another partnership shares skilled volunteer opportunities posted on VolunteerMatch with another 10 million professionals through LinkedIn's Volunteer Marketplace. Figure 2.1 demonstrates VolunteerMatch's "Reach."

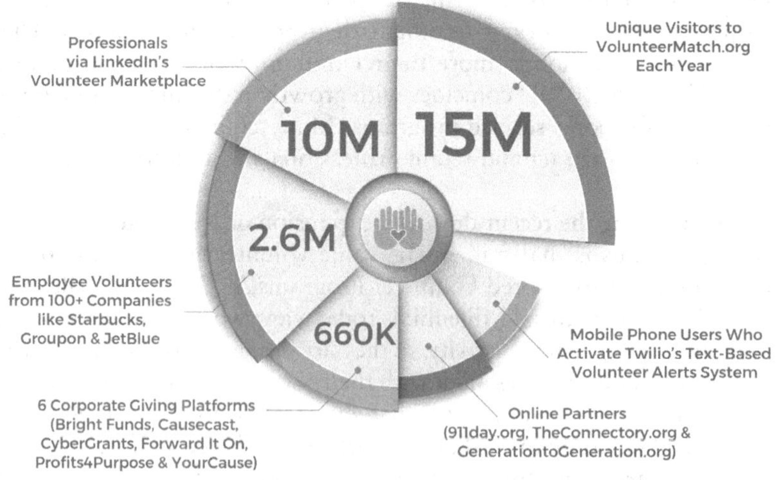

FIGURE 2.1. VolunteerMatch "Reach"

Trend 5: Technology Advances

Online Recruitment

You may be familiar with recruiting volunteers online. Sites such as VolunteerMatch.org, DoSomething.org, the Points of Light Foundation's HandsOn Network, and the federal site Serve.gov provide a place for organizations to post their volunteer opportunities and be connected with potential volunteers. LinkedIn also has an option for their members to be offered options to volunteer.

The advantage of online recruitment sites is that they extend your reach far beyond your current recruitment methods and definitely beyond who you know. If you haven't already added an online strategy to your repertoire of recruitment options, you should definitely consider it.

More about online recruitment and how to use it can be found in Chapter 4, "Volunteer Recruitment."

Virtual Volunteers

Virtual volunteers complete their volunteer assignment—all or a portion—via the Internet on their home or work computer. Research for a grant proposal or newsletter, translating documents into another language, or designing a newsletter, brochure, or logo, for example, can be done by someone with those skills on the other side of town or on the other side of the country. You may never even meet them face-to-face. A great place to see examples of possible virtual volunteer positions such as research, translation, and many more is the UN Volunteers site.[19]

This strategy also allows volunteers to participate who might not be able to be onsite due to a disability or their work schedule.

Virtual volunteerism is a great strategy for everyone but may be particularly useful to libraries in small or rural communities. The ability to seek professional skills beyond your service area may vastly expand your options.

REAL-LIFE EXAMPLE: VIRTUAL VOLUNTEER

Amy Campbell, reference librarian at the Marshall Public Library, in Pocatello, Idaho, shared her story:

> We connected with a skilled virtual volunteer who does fund-raising and grant writing for us all the way from North Carolina.
>
> Audrey came across our VolunteerMatch posting for an experienced grant-writing volunteer. This was a posting I'd had up for a few years without getting any good results, but Audrey fit the bill. She had been an educational nonprofit director for 10 years, and during that time had done plenty of fund-raising and grant writing. She had a robust background in event planning and networking, which was kind of the icing on the volunteer cake.
>
> She found the listing just as she was searching for an opportunity to give back and even though we're a few thousand miles apart and we've never met in person, over the past year, she's given about 100 hours of her time to help this community in Idaho that she had never even heard of before.[20]

Audrey Smith, in North Carolina, is serving Amy's Idaho library as a virtual volunteer. She told this story about her experience:

> Audrey's grandparents were lifelong examples of quiet volunteerism, and her mother also always encouraged her to get involved, ensuring that Audrey grew up loving it, and has been an active volunteer her whole life.
>
> As a journalist and former director of a nonprofit, she has writing and grant-writing skills to share. She moved to North Carolina two years ago, and wanted a volunteer connection, so she went to VolunteerMatch.org and entered her skills as search criteria. The virtual grant-writer opportunity at the Marshall Public Library in Idaho caught her eye.

She went through the same interview process as if she had been interviewing for a job because they were looking for someone very experienced. It was a little daunting and seemed a bit scary until she talked to Amy on the phone, and cleared up her concerns. It was reassuring to learn that she wouldn't be "signing away her life."

The two do all their work via e-mail and phone. Although they've never met, they have developed a library program called "Books into Boxes." They partner with the Idaho Food Bank to include books in the Thanksgiving food boxes distributed to families in need, providing new books to expand home libraries for the children.

They worked together to define what each of their roles would be. Audrey contacts publishers and authors to request donations of new books and has written a grant to help the library leverage its discount purchasing power to buy even more. Amy made the connection with the Food Bank, accepts the donated books, and writes the thank you notes on the library's letterhead.

While she had volunteered at her local library back home, Audrey had not been a virtual volunteer, like she is now. She says her time is easier spent as a single parent doing her volunteer work by sharing her skills from her home computer. She's driven by the issues she wants to support, and in addition to the library, has taken on a similar position with a second organization.

Describing herself as a lifelong learner, Audrey says "volunteering benefits you no matter how busy you are because it enriches your life and gives you perspective. It's important to be part of something bigger than yourself. You learn so much, so you make time to do the work." She says she's learned a lot about literacy while working on the Books into Boxes project with the library.

Audrey is also creating the next generation of volunteers. Having home schooled her children, she's always impressed on them the importance of leaving the world a better place, and she says they're already following in her footsteps.[21]

"Many people actively search for volunteer opportunities they can complete via home or work computers, because of time constraints, personal preference, a disability or a home-based obligation that prevents them from volunteering on-site. Virtual volunteering allows anyone to contribute time and expertise . . . from his or her home or office."[22]

Online Meeting Technologies

Platforms like Webex, ReadyTalk, and GoToMeeting allow you to meet with people online in real time from their home or office. You can see a person or multiple people, talk to them, review materials or websites together—you can even put a group together for orientation, training, or a focus group.

This technology is especially useful in rural areas where travel consumes time and money or is impossible due to weather or terrain. In today's world, however, you don't have to be rural to benefit from this technology. If you have traffic or public transportation issues, or even if people are just busy, online meetings can be a solution. Most of them even allow you to record the meeting for playback later by those who couldn't attend live.

If access to one of these online platforms has eluded your budget, it's worth taking a look at TechSoup.org, a nonprofit providing low- or no-cost technology resources to libraries and nonprofits.

Micro-Volunteering

Micro-volunteering takes virtual volunteering a step further. As described by HelpFromHome.org, through micro-volunteering you can "Volunteer your time in bite sized chunks, from your own home, on demand and on your own terms. Benefit worthy causes to suit your lifestyle via non-skilled actions. Dip in and dip out with absolutely no commitment."[23]

The HelpFromHome site offers volunteer projects based on skills you'd like to share or gain such as writing, data entry, research, analysis, translation, or creative pursuits, among others.

Heather Sturgess, author of "Micro-Volunteering: Worth the Hype?," decided to try micro-volunteering to see if she could really make any kind of difference from home and on short notice: "I was surprised at the range of activities available and the different tasks I was able to contribute to. In one evening I counted penguins in the Antarctic, and identified animals in the Serengeti without leaving my sofa. I enjoyed working on the different projects; the activities were really straight forward and made me curious to learn more about these organisations and investigate for myself. Conveniently, the projects provided links to more information, so I dived in. To my surprise, I actually made a contribution by looking at pictures of cute penguins and learning about animals in the Serengeti. These animal micro-volunteering projects help scientists monitor ecosystems and track changes in species population and breeding overtime to help inform conservation policies."[24]

REAL-LIFE EXAMPLE: MICRO-VOLUNTEERING

The Smithsonian Digital Volunteers Transcription Center,[25] as of this writing, engages over 8,000 volunteers in projects from transcribing comedian Phyllis Diller's "Gag File" (a collection of more than 50,000 jokes), to the Smithsonian Tropical Research Institute–Center for Tropical Paleoecology and Archaeology's need for transcription of specimen cards for the pollen collection. Each card corresponds to a microscope slide of a grain of pollen, and the transcription of the data helps researchers in their work.

This concept won't be for everyone, but it does provide some insight into the kinds of things volunteers are interested in, and can do from afar. If you have a collection of historical photographs that need to be described or tagged, for example, or a special local genealogy collection you need help with, this approach might be useful.

Social Media and Volunteering

The National Museum of American History posted a call for volunteers on Facebook to help with transcription of the Phyllis Diller "Gag File."[26] It caught my attention, and I quickly shared it with my 300+ friends, as well as in this book. Sharing volunteer stories and opportunities across a variety of social media will extend your reach and attract interested people.

The extent to which you will use social media for this will very much depend on the resources you have available, as it takes time and people to create good content to share and post regularly. But at least consider starting small. If your library already has a Facebook page, blog, or Twitter feed, don't miss an opportunity to share a great story about volunteering at the library, then encourage your volunteers and staff to share those posts on their own social media accounts. Their friends will be more interested if they know someone who's already involved. You might also think of a role for volunteers to play in helping you expand your social media efforts.

REAL-LIFE EXAMPLE: WHERE THE NEED FOR SOCIAL MEDIA ASSISTANCE, ONLINE RECRUITING, VIRTUAL VOLUNTEERING, AND ONLINE MEETING TECHNOLOGY CONVERGED

To demonstrate the power of these new technologies in volunteer engagement, here's a real-life volunteer example from my own experience:

> The goals of the Facebook page for the California State Library's statewide literacy program were to raise awareness about adult literacy and to recruit potential volunteer tutors. I learned to use Facebook—even

Facebook ads—but that was the extent of my social media expertise. Wanting to expand beyond what I knew and had time for, I created a "social media specialist" volunteer position, and posted it on Volunteer Match.org.

The person selected after interviews was an e-commerce professional—a millennial—specializing in social media and e-mail marketing, who had just moved to town for a new job. As a newcomer to her company, she was uncomfortable committing to a volunteer position that would take time away from her workday.

This volunteer position interested her knowing that most of her volunteering could be done online at home. And since her new job focused on e-mail marketing to the exclusion of social media, an added benefit to her was the opportunity to keep her hand in the social media world, while volunteering for a cause she could support in her new community.

To accommodate her new job, we did our interview, and all of our work together on an online meeting platform during her lunch hour. She served as a virtual volunteer, providing insights and advice that were invaluable, and created some outstanding content to post, which helped to increase our reach.

We never actually met in person until the end of our work together when I asked her if she would be willing to be videotaped about her experience for our website![27]

Trend 6: Collaboration with Other Organizations

Strategic Collaborations

Consider some ways that the library could partner with another organization to benefit both: Do you ever need someone to oversee small children while parents are involved in a program at the library? Or someone to read or do crafts with young children? If so, consider partnering with a junior high- or high school-aged Girl Scout troop. They often need to earn community service hours—and, they come with adult leadership!

How about a local Lions or Kiwanis Club looking for a project to engage their members in? Or a local college seeking community volunteer opportunities for their students, a farmers' market that wants to plant a community garden or start a seed bank, or a local historical society or genealogy club whose members would enjoy helping library users with classes or one-on-one assistance?

McKnight and Kretzmann[28] suggest that "libraries can work together with community leaders to connect their library in a vital web of mutually beneficial relationships . . . they will be able to form creative partnerships with parks, artists and cultural institutions, police departments, senior citizen's organizations, and a wide variety of other local individuals, organizations and institutions."

The "asset map" graphic shown in Figure 2.2[29] provides some examples of the kinds of things that can be exchanged in mutually beneficial relationships between the library and a variety of potential community partners.

FIGURE 2.2. One-on-One Relationships (*Source:* John P. Kretzmanna and John L. McKnight, "One on One Relationships," from *Building Communities from the Inside Out,* Chart 3, p. 204. Evanston IL: Center for Urban Affairs and Policy Research, Northwestern University, 1993.)

From the Urban Libraries Council: "Libraries . . . can truly build community. They come to the table with a wealth of assets: free community space, connections to the local economy, a sense of ownership by the community, and, above all, a level of community trust. With these assets, they can connect to all parts of a community, building those relationships and networks that contribute to social capital. They can make policy makers into avid supporters. They can be network catalysts and community players."[30]

As with any relationship, it's important to listen to the potential partner's needs and not just focus solely on yours. The best and longest-lasting collaborations are those in which both parties receive benefits. You'll find the best opportunities for partnering by looking at where your needs and goals intersect with a potential collaborator's needs and goals.

Consider reaching out to an organization you've strategically identified to engage the specific skills of their members. For example, when recruiting skilled trainers as volunteers to deliver a workshop curriculum we devised, the local chapter of the American Society for Training & Development (now known as ATD—the Association for Talent Development) was the strategic choice for collaboration. They were happy to refer their members who were interested in sharing their skills as volunteers in the community, while gaining additional training experience.

It was important that these volunteers came to us with documented training skills in order to achieve the highest quality delivery of the information. We could teach volunteers who had successful training experience the workshop content but lacked the time and skills to teach someone with little expertise or experience to be an effective trainer.

If you have a high-skilled volunteer position you're trying to recruit for, consider identifying a professional association that represents that skill. Did you know there's a Public Relations Society of America? And seven graphic design associations? You can find these and other associations that might meet your needs in the *Encyclopedia of Associations,* which can be found in many libraries' Reference collection.

Local Volunteer Support Organizations

In many communities, you will be able to find entire organizations that are in business to help you find volunteers, and some even provide training and support for staff who engage and support volunteers.

Volunteer Centers and HandsOn Networks—not-for-profits themselves—aim to increase volunteerism. They gather organizations' job descriptions, reach out into the community for potential volunteers, and refer qualified people for interviews. Many also provide training and/or problem-solving help on volunteer engagement. Your local United Way may also provide this service or be able to tell you who does in your area.

In addition, some communities have organized local professional associations for volunteer engagement professionals to meet periodically to share ideas and problem solve. Often called DOVIAs (Directors of Volunteers in Agencies), a list is maintained by state.[31]

Some city and county governments also offer volunteer recruitment services to their departments, so if your library is a part of your local government, be sure to participate where that is available. Examples include the city of Sacramento, California, and Washington County, Oregon.[32]

CHAPTER SUMMARY

The purpose of this chapter is to highlight changing demographics and volunteerism trends that provide insight for planning and implementing volunteer engagement successfully. Considering these ideas and tools as you design your approach can help you recruit the right volunteers and watch them grow into powerful library supporters and advocates.

NOTES

1. Johnson, Megan, and Larry Johnson, *Generations, Inc.* (American Management Association, 2010), p. 6.
2. "Issue Brief: Baby Boomers and Volunteering: Findings from Corporation Research," Corporation for National & Community Service, March 2007. https://www.nationalservice.gov/sites/default/files/documents/boomer_research.pdf (accessed March 5, 2017).
3. "Reinventing Aging: Baby Boomers and Civic Engagement," Harvard School of Public Health, MetLife Foundation, 2004. http://assets.aarp.org/rgcenter/general/boomers_engagement.pdf (accessed March 5, 2017).
4. "Great Expectations: Boomers and the Future of Volunteering," VolunteerMatch.org, 2006. https://www.volunteermatch.org/nonprofits/resources/greatexpectations (accessed March 5, 2017).
5. "Millennials Want to Make a Serious Impact and You Can Help," Catchafireblog.org, March 10, 2014. https://catchafireblog.org/millennials-want-to-make-a-serious-impact-and-you-can-help-7927c561c17d#.prvqs72qd (accessed March 5, 2017).
6. Crosby, Jackie, "As Older Minnesota Volunteers Leave, Who Will Replace Them?" Star Tribune, 2015. http://www.startribune.com/as-older-minnesota-volunteers-leave-who-will-replace-them/289739831 (accessed March 3, 2017).
7. Corporation for National and Community Service, "Volunteering and Civic Life in America," 2015. https://www.nationalservice.gov/vcla/demographic (accessed March 3, 2017).
8. The Millennial Impact Project. www.themillennialimpact.com (accessed March 3, 2017).
9. "The Millennial Impact Report Retrospective: Five Years of Trends," November 2016. http://www.themillennialimpact.com/research (accessed March 3, 2017).

10. Geiger, Abigail, "Millennials Are the Most Likely Generation of Americans to Use Public Libraries," 2017. http://www.pewresearch.org/fact-tank/2017/06/21/millennials-are-the-most-likely-generation-of-americans-to-use-public-libraries (accessed October 18, 2017).

11. If you would like to see the public relations specialist volunteer describe why he took this volunteer position in a 6-minute video, you'll find it here: https://www.youtube.com/watch?v=CmjRBxOmoUc&feature=youtu.be (accessed March 26, 2017).

12. Rosenthal, Robert J., Ed., *Volunteer Engagement 2.0: Ideas and Insights Changing the World* (Hoboken, NJ: Wiley & Sons, 2015), p. 199.

13. Young, Joan, "Volunteer Engagement: Changing Your Volunteer Culture," Urban Libraries Council, 2012. http://www.urbanlibraries.org/volunteer-engagement—changing-our-volunteer-culture-innovation-34.php?page_id=41 (accessed March 9, 2017).

14. Chart information adapted from Jill Friedman Fixler, *Boomer Volunteer Engagement: Collaborate Today, Thrive Tomorrow* (Bloomington, IN: Author House, 2008).

15. Rosenthal, *Volunteer Engagement 2.0,* p. 15.

16. University of Washington Center for Leadership and Social Responsibility, http://www.corporatesocialresponsibility.com (accessed March 6, 2017).

17. Parmar, Neil, "A Different Kind of Volunteer Work," 2017. https://www.wsj.com/articles/a-different-kind-of-volunteer-work-1505095922 (accessed October 19, 2017).

18. "Why Company Sponsored Volunteer Programs Are Keeping Millennials Happy at Work," Forbes, September 22, 2016. https://www.forbes.com/sites/kaytiezimmerman/2016/09/22/company-sponsored-volunteer-programs-are-keeping-millennials-happy/#9e60b5a78da9 (accessed October 18, 2017).

19. https://www.onlinevolunteering.org/en/opportunities.

20. Comments of Amy Campbell, reference librarian, Marshall Public Library, Pocatello, Idaho, via e-mail, March 2017.

21. Comments of Audrey M. Smith, virtual volunteer for the Marshall Public Library, Pocatello, Idaho, via phone interview, March 20, 2017.

22. RGK Center for Philanthropy and Community Service, University of Texas at Austin. www.serviceleader.org/virtual (accessed March 7, 2017).

23. www.helpfromhome.org (accessed March 7, 2017).

24. Sturgess, Heather, "Micro-Volunteering: Worth the Hype?" August 2016. https://nfpsynergy.net/blog/micro-volunteering-worth-hype (accessed September 27, 2017).

25. Smithsonian Digital Volunteers Transcription Center. https://transcription.si.edu (accessed March 12, 2017).

26. National Museum of American History, Phyllis Diller "Gag File." http://americanhistory.si.edu/blog/help-us-transcribe-phyllis-dillers-jokes (accessed September 25, 2017).

27. If you would like to see the social media volunteer describe why she took this volunteer position in a 4-minute video, you'll find it here: https://getinvolvedclearinghouse.org/resource/training-materials/skilled-volunteer-interview-social-media-specialist (accessed February 13, 2018).

28. McKnight, John, and John Kretzmann, *Building Communities from the Inside Out: A Path toward Finding and Mobilizing a Community's Assets* (Evanston IL: Center for Urban Affairs and Policy Research, Northwestern University, 1993).

29. Ibid.

30. Urban Libraries Council, Kretzmann, Jody, and Susan Rans, *The Engaged Library: Chicago Stories of Community Building* (Washington, D.C.: Urban Libraries Council, 2005), p. 6.

31. Energize Inc. www.energizeinc.com/prof/dovia.html (accessed March 30, 2017).

32. City of Sacramento (CA): http://www.cityofsacramento.org/HR/Volunteer-Opportunities (accessed March 12, 2017). Washington County (OR) volunteer links: http://www.co.washington.or.us/Volunteers/Volunteer-Links.cfm (accessed March 12, 2017).

3

Why People Volunteer

MOTIVATION

The most often asked question about volunteering has to be: "How do you motivate volunteers?" To answer that, we must begin by asking a critically important question: "Why do people volunteer?"

Start with what makes *you* want to volunteer. My reasons for volunteering include:

- I volunteered at my daughter's schools over the years to familiarize myself with the people and the place she was surrounded by most of the day.
- I volunteer with the Girl Scouts because I want there to be more strong women leaders in our society and because it's given me a common interest and quality time with my daughter. An added benefit has been the friends I've met along the way.
- I'm a skilled trainer and often volunteer my training skills when that's an option.
- I've volunteered for the National Humpback Whale Marine Sanctuary's annual whale count program because it generates information that helps scientists support the whale population, because I learn more about whales through the training provided, and because it gives me a chance (and an excuse!) to sit by the ocean and watch whales for 4 solid gloriously uninterrupted hours.

Susan J. Ellis, president of Energize, Inc., provides a pretty comprehensive list of the of reasons that people volunteer.[1] A few of her examples include to feel needed, to share a skill, to learn something new, and to demonstrate a commitment to a cause.

"Volunteers want to know what is in it for them, be it career-experience, a life-changing experience or a chance to use their skills, build team morale or make friends. Volunteering experiences that fail to take these motives into account or respect that a placement is a two-way street will always be a struggle to fill and remain high in turnover."[2]

So, here's the answer to the question "How do we motivate volunteers?" *The answer is that we don't.* Volunteer motivation doesn't appear based on something we do *to them*. They come with a motivation that we need to understand. We must identify their reason(s) for volunteering and determine the right volunteer job for them—the one that satisfies their motivation and meets our need. That's our role in volunteer motivation.

Most often people will say their reason for volunteering is to "give back" or to support an organization or service that's important to them. That is usually a true statement, and while *very* important, there is usually another reason for volunteering.

If they are only asked, "What would you like to do?"—most will say they're happy to do "Whatever you need done." They don't mean it, however. Without knowing the options, they don't know what would be a good fit. You must uncover their skills and interests, as well as their reason for volunteering, and then offer them a volunteer job that meets your need *and theirs*.

Volunteers who are new to the community may be motivated by wanting to meet people, for example. If you give them a shelving job, they'll feel isolated and won't meet anyone. So one of these things will happen: (1) after their first or second shift, they'll stop coming, or (2) they'll begin to chat with staff and volunteers and become a major distraction. Placing them in a job that allowed them to meet people in the first place would have saved you from having to deal with the disruption, and most likely have saved a volunteer whose interests and skills would have been beneficial to the library elsewhere.

And the reverse—giving an assignment that entails working with the public to someone who chose the library for its opportunity to have some quiet and solitude—is also a bad move.

If volunteers really have no idea what they'd like to do, it's your responsibility to identify their skills and interests in order to make a good match. No matter how much people say they want to volunteer for the library, if they are unhappy in the job they've been assigned, they won't stay.

Volunteers who stop showing up or disappear shortly after the carefully developed training you provided are probably unhappy in the job and just aren't sure how to express that to you.

When we are in dire need of volunteers for a particular job, sometimes the needs and interests of the volunteer get overlooked. The result is that many opportunities and volunteers are lost.

When the volunteers are happy, they will more likely to be successful. And when volunteers are successful, so are the library's volunteer engagement efforts, as are the people overseeing them. Volunteers will more likely be successful when they are given the right job—the one that matches the reasons they wanted to volunteer in the first place.

Remember, they didn't come to you so that they could be *un*successful at something, and they're not sharing their precious time just to make work for you. They came because they (1) wanted to make a difference and (2) because they have another reason you must make it your business to find out.

WHY WRITTEN VOLUNTEER JOB DESCRIPTIONS?

Understanding volunteer motivation is critical to your success, and crafting well thought out volunteer job descriptions is your highest priority task. Carefully designed job descriptions help you place the right volunteer in each job, avoid turnover, and improve the chance that goals will be achieved.

The job description is a planning tool that is the building block for success in all aspects of volunteer engagement. Read on and find out why.

Job Description Reason 1: Clarifies Roles

Tensions can arise when staff members think that volunteers are "going too far" or that they're "not doing enough." If volunteers are clear about the responsibilities of the staff and other volunteers working around them, they are less likely to step on anyone's toes. Volunteers shouldn't have to *guess* what their responsibilities and limits of authority are, because their guess probably won't be the same as what you had in mind.

Volunteer job descriptions that are clearly articulated clarify roles and responsibilities—where they begin and end—and aid in the relationship between staff and volunteers.

Job Description Reason 2: Serves as Your Primary Recruitment and Placement Tool

A well-developed job description gives you a leg up on determining who you're looking for because you've outlined the qualifications required and responsibilities of the position. And, knowing all that helps you know where to find them. When you review the job description with the potential volunteer, you will both be better prepared to decide whether or not it's a good fit.

Job Description Reason 3: Basis for Feedback and Support

When a volunteer can read a job description and make the decision to accept or not accept an assignment, rather than just being provided a verbal description, it will be easier to address any performance concerns that arise. If issues come up, revisiting the written job description will reinforce the initial conversation and agreement.

Job Description Reason 4: Serves as an Agreement

Although it by no means implies a formal contract, some organizations elect to include a signature line for the volunteers at the bottom, signifying that they understand what they've agreed to do. This might make it more likely that they actually read it before saying yes, and increase the odds that they commit to it when they do.

Job Description Reason 5: Prevents Common Problems

Carefully crafted job descriptions are critical planning and recruitment tools. The process of thinking through a complete volunteer job description forces you to plan: Who will this position be working with? How much time will it take? What skills are required? As a result of this planning process, and once it's in writing, expectations can be clearly communicated.

Bring staff in to help plan for and design volunteer job descriptions that relate to their programs or areas of the library. This provides you with a clearer picture of what's needed for the job and helps to gain staff "buy-in" for the concept because they've had the opportunity to give input on how it should work.

This process forces both you, and the staff, to truly define where it fits in the organizational structure, what qualifications a volunteer will need to be successful, and what training will be required. Knowing all of that will also go a long way to help you recruit the best person for each assignment.

DESIGNING GOOD VOLUNTEER JOB DESCRIPTIONS

What should be included in a good job description, and why? Let's review an example. In the Appendices for this chapter you'll find a job description for a "public speaker" volunteer. This was developed with a library that was getting ready to do a major fund-raising campaign and wanted to reach out to community groups in advance with information about the library, but you could use it for any reason you have to get the word out—a newly launched service, for example, or to recruit potential volunteers.

Here's a walk through the format:

Title

Don't make the job title "volunteer"—instead, the title should describe the specific role the volunteer will play. "Public speaker" clues the potential volunteer in at the outset as to what the job will be. The volunteer can quickly decide if he or she wants to read the whole thing or not.

Position Overview and Impact

In this section, don't describe *what* the volunteer would do, but instead give him or her an understanding of *why* the position is important. What difference will it make if someone volunteers to do this? Are there meaningful outcomes of giving his or her precious time to this task? Help the potential volunteer understand how the job is meaningful.

The position overview and impact statement for the public speaker job clearly articulates its value—they're going to be helping to raise awareness about what the library has to offer to attract people to use its resources, and reach out to potential volunteers and supporters.

Another good example of a meaningful overview and impact statement is for volunteer book menders. Though you may see the outcome of this job as "cleaning the grunge off books," that sounds unimportant until you describe the real difference it makes to library patrons, which is "to keep the best-loved books available for patron use."

A caution here is not to make the impact statement about helping the library staff, but about kids who want to check out *Curious George* and *The Hungry Hungry Caterpillar.*

Key Responsibilities

This is where you tell the potential volunteers what will be expected of them, what tasks they'll have responsibility for, and who they'll be working with. Some job descriptions only contain a list of tasks, but that doesn't give the full picture—it's only part of the information a potential volunteer needs in order to make a good decision.

The key responsibilities also help potential volunteers begin to either picture themselves doing this work, or not. In this case, they will be given the information they need for their public speaking engagements and won't have to create the presentations by themselves. They get an orientation to the library, as well as a prepared outline and materials. Do you see how this could reduce their hesitance about taking this job?

They can also see that they can accept or reject speaking engagements when asked, based on their schedule—that answers a big question for them. And finally, they see they'll be making a brief report on the experience within three days—including any questions they were unable to answer at the time. This reduces the volunteers' anxiety knowing that if they don't know the answer to a question asked by the group, there is a plan to follow up with the information. That wraps up their concerns nicely.

Qualifications

Here, you define what skills and characteristics are required for a volunteer to be successful in the position. The public speaker must already have successful public speaking skills. Volunteers without those qualifications will take themselves out of the running here, if they haven't already.

For volunteers to be successful, you must define in advance what will be required of them. Providing a clear understanding of the requirements will help them (*and* you) make the right decision about whether or not this is the job for them.

Training and Support Provided

What needs to be done in order to prepare volunteers for this position? In this section, you're signaling to the volunteer, "Don't worry—if you've got the qualifications listed above, we'll provide you with the rest of the information you need." Here you identify what training will be provided—in this case an orientation to the library, and the materials—and that you have backup support from someone—in this case, access to the speaker's bureau coordinator if needed. This not only reduces potential volunteer's anxiety about being able to do the job successfully or not, but it also sends a message that you're serious enough about this volunteer assignment that you'll spend time training the person and be available to answer questions.

Time Commitment

One of the first questions a volunteer has when asked to volunteer is "How much time will it take?" So, state in the description how many hours per week or month are expected—make your best estimate. Volunteers can then make a conscious decision and determine if the time commitment required can realistically fit into their schedule.

Commitment Length

Define the length of time that's expected. Do you need six months, a year? Say so. The message conveyed by delineating the length of time you need is that this position is very important. And since we already described the training that will be provided, the potential volunteer knows you'll be investing time and resources preparing him or her for the position, so before you bring the person in, you'll need a serious commitment.

Putting a time commitment in the job description also provides an end date. The volunteers can see they won't need to feel guilty after completing that time commitment if they decide to move on. By saying "minimum commitment requested," you're also saying that if they do that first six months, and want to continue, there's an opportunity to do so. Not including a specific length of time you're seeking gives the impression this will be an open-ended time period—the potential volunteers will perceive it as every Monday afternoon for the rest of their life! People won't say yes if that's their impression. They like to know there's an end if they want one.

Staff will be comforted seeing a specific length of commitment identified because they're concerned it won't work anyway.

Delineating a potential end date also gives you and the staff that amount of time for training and coaching the volunteer—time enough to find out if it's the right fit. At the end of that time period you can say, "You know, we tried this, but it doesn't seem to be working out for you. Why don't we look for another assignment that's a better fit." The "other assignment" could be another position in your library, or somewhere else in the community. Just don't wait for the time period to be up before coaching begins if there's an issue or concern with the volunteer. Give the volunteer a chance to succeed with your help. If he or she can't, start the transition to a new position—or out the door—before the time commitment is up.

Benefits of Volunteering

This job description section is very important, but, unfortunately, it's often not included. What does the volunteer stand to gain from engaging in this role? This section helps the volunteer match his or her motivation for volunteering with a job that satisfies it. Perhaps one benefit is to meet people. Maybe it's the opportunity to share a skill or learn a new one. The important thing is that you've designed a job that does have benefits to the volunteer, and you articulate them here.

For the volunteer public speaker, the benefits are helping the library and the community by utilizing skills he or she already has, and developing new contacts.

This is a very important planning piece and must be considered carefully. Outlining what a volunteer might gain from taking the assignment will help determine recruiting strategy. Knowing the kind of person you're looking for will give you ideas about where to look.

If you can't think of any benefits for a volunteer job, then it may not be a volunteer job—this may be something you either have to pay someone to do, or you could consider assigning court-appointed volunteers to it if you have a program like that in your community.

And while the following benefits to volunteers probably won't appear on your written job descriptions, it's good for you to know that volunteering can lead to both job search and health benefits.

LinkedIn reports that 41 percent of those on LinkedIn, in a position to hire, consider volunteer experience just as valuable as paid work experience; 20 percent agree they have hired candidates because of their volunteer work experience; and 27 percent of job seekers are more likely to be hired, when unemployed, if they volunteer."[3]

In addition to overall health benefits, it's been shown that volunteering can help to improve self-esteem, promote longevity, reduce the risk of Alzheimer's, and improve school and college experience.[4,5]

Ongoing Library Contact

Who is the person the volunteers will be working most closely with? Who do they notify if they're going on vacation? If they're having a problem, or have a question, who do they talk to? Having an understanding of these relationships will be comforting to the volunteers.

Location

Where will the volunteer activities take place? At one library location, or several? In this case, after training, most of the work will happen out in the community where the public speaking takes place. In the case of a volunteer assignment that can be done virtually—from the volunteer's own computer, home, or workplace—that would be outlined here.

Date Revised

If you want to be sure you're always using the most updated version of the job description, remember to date it.

Initial Contact Person

Who does one contact to inquire about this position? Providing, name, title, phone, and e-mail is best.

Grounds for Termination

Although it may not be necessary to state grounds for termination in each job description, it can be useful in specific situations.

One example is confidentiality. If a volunteer will be working around information that must be kept confidential, a very clear way to suggest how important keeping confidentiality is to the library is to state on the job description and discuss in the interview and during training that breaking confidentiality will lead to termination of the volunteer. Volunteer programs in all types of organizations successfully require a confidentiality commitment from their volunteers—hospitals, child abuse and domestic violence programs, schools, and libraries. Those that are successful are those that make both expectations and consequences clearly understood from the beginning.

Other grounds for termination for volunteers might be disregarding policies that define appropriate interactions with children, or with homebound patrons. Raising these very important issues in a "Grounds for Termination" section of specific volunteer job descriptions goes a long way toward making it exceedingly clear how important they are.

JOB DESCRIPTION TIPS

Tip 1: Don't Write Them without Input from Others

Engage staff and volunteers who will work with this position, or who already do the job. Input from them will improve your characterization, and including them in the design of the job description will help ensure their acceptance for this volunteer role.

If you need additional help crafting good job descriptions, consider staff who share this role from surrounding libraries or other community organizations doing volunteer engagement work, like someone from the Red Cross or the SPCA. They may feel isolated too, and be glad to get together on the phone or over a cup of coffee to review a job description you're creating, and you can return the favor.

Tip 2: Be Sure What You've Written Is Realistic

Once you've finished writing, take a good hard look at it. Realistically, would a volunteer accept this job, or does it describe a position for a full-time employee? Even if you could find someone to volunteer on a full-time basis, that's not a good idea. You could become very dependent on that person, and when that volunteer leaves, or his or her schedule no longer permits the same number of hours, remember that if it's important to continue the work the volunteer was doing, you will inherit it.

If what you've described does look more like a role for a full-time employee, try breaking it apart into two or more assignments that could fit together to get the job done.

Tip 3: Include Enough Information to Recruit the Right Person

Have you included enough information in the job description to help you find the right volunteer? Have you described thoroughly the qualifications required? Are benefits to the volunteer clearly articulated? How much time is needed and over what period?

If what's in your head is not on the page, it will be difficult for someone else to understand and respond.

Tip 4: Think Strategically: What Do You Need?

Don't start with what you think you can get. Instead, think about what you *need* to serve your community the way you want to serve it. Do you need computer coaches? Homework helpers? An assistant to help with volunteer recruitment or data management? Don't understate what you want. Write a job description to address what you need.

Then think about who could do this job. Does it have to be an individual? Or could it be done by a couple of volunteers or a small team sharing the workload? Is there a local service club, corporation, or small business that could do all or part of it? How about a virtual volunteer?

Tip 5: Consider Creating Some Program Management Positions for Volunteers

As the number of volunteer jobs you offer and number of volunteers increase, consider delegating to skilled and qualified volunteers some of the volunteer coordination responsibilities. The speaker's bureau coordinator position in the Appendices for this chapter is a companion job description to the public speaker example used earlier in this chapter. The speaker's bureau coordinator volunteer will be overseeing the speaker's bureau on your behalf—recruiting and training the public speaker volunteers as well as securing speaking engagements with community groups and scheduling a trained public speaker to attend. They will even track and report volunteer hours and presentation statistics quarterly.

This job has additional qualifications beyond those of the public speaker—it requires project management skills as well as someone who already has some contacts in the community. And while not *every* public speaker is qualified to be the speaker's bureau coordinator, if you do find one that does have the qualifications, this is a potential "promotion" for that volunteer—a way to not only say thanks, but to reward the volunteer with a higher level position if the person would like it. And since this job reports to the library's director, it's identified as a very important one.

Think about how you can use the examples here to create your own management positions for volunteers that help to address the need for meaningful work for volunteers to do, opportunities for volunteers to use their skills, chances to offer a promotion to a high-performing skilled volunteer, and an opportunity to reduce the workload for the volunteer engagement staff, which allows them to use that time to move on to designing the next volunteer engagement adventure. (For more on this idea, see Chapter 6, "How It All Gets Done," in the section "Avoiding Burnout of the Volunteer Engagement Coordinator.")

REAL-LIFE EXAMPLE: MANAGEMENT POSITIONS FOR VOLUNTEERS

The Monrovia Public Library (California) built a "Volunteer Management Team" with three individual volunteers working together to manage a variety of responsibilities to support the staff member tasked as the library's volunteer engagement coordinator for part of her time.

The first volunteer member of the team oversees the library's "computer coaches." She established an e-mail list for all the coaches to get to know each other, share common questions they get to improve their support of their customers, and request a substitute should they be unable to keep an assigned shift. She also set up a Google calendar to help with managing volunteers' shifts and ensure coverage.

The role of the second volunteer on the team is to get to know the staff and their needs and supply volunteers for their events, including volunteers to work in the Friends' bookstore. She, along with other members of the team, coordinates volunteer recognition.

The third team member is a volunteer tutor in the library's adult literacy program. Her job is to reach out to all the volunteer literacy tutors on a monthly basis to answer questions, provide support, and help them feel connected. She also collects their monthly report information.[6]

Tip 6: Delegate Part of the Volunteer Engagement Duties to Volunteers

Staff charged with the responsibility for volunteer engagement can expand their reach by engaging competent volunteers in clearly defined tasks that must be done to ensure good volunteer engagement.

As time goes on, you'll uncover many more exciting ways to engage volunteers in the library's work. One way to protect yourself from getting stretched too thin or even burned out is to consider delegating some tasks in the volunteer engagement office to qualified volunteers.

REAL-LIFE EXAMPLE: ASSISTANT VOLUNTEER COORDINATOR

When we embraced the volunteer engagement philosophy at the California State Library, responsibility for managing that work and guiding our internal team fell to me, on top of my already full workload. It quickly became apparent that I would need assistance in order to do everything we wanted to do.

A good tool for identifying what help you need is to think about your full workload as a pie, determining which "slices" don't have to be specifically done by you, which you don't have the appropriate skills for, and which are not your favorites. Then, design volunteer job descriptions that will take on those slices of the pie.

In the Appendices for this chapter you'll find a job description for "assistant volunteer coordinator." Reviewing it will help to see how this is done:

Title: Assistant Volunteer Coordinator

The title has a professional sound to it—thus a benefit to someone who would like to use it on a résumé. It also makes clear through use of the word "assistant" that the responsibility would not be the applicant's alone.

Position Overview and Impact

This section clues the potential volunteers into what the position is, while clearly stating the impact their work will have: "Supports the engagement of volunteers to assist in achieving the state library's information and cultural heritage mission, and increase the library's visibility and community connections."

Key Responsibilities

Monitoring our VolunteerMatch account was quickly identified as a potential task for delegation because it required attention several times per week. It was also something that could be done by someone besides me once the person was trained. Identifying the most qualified applicants by comparing applications to job description was a task that would also be very helpful, and if possible, having this person join our internal volunteer engagement team would help him or her learn about our goals and procedures, while sharing experiences and data with the group.

Qualifications

We were looking for someone who shared our values related to volunteerism, and potentially someone who wanted to learn about volunteer engagement practices. The person would need good communication and organizational skills, as well as the ability to maintain confidentiality. It would be helpful to have a human resources background if possible, but we decided it wasn't a requirement.

Training and Support Provided

This section of the job description clarified that the applicant would receive training, so he or she didn't have to already know everything when the person walked through the door, and would also have access to staff as needed for coordination, questions, and problem solving.

Time and Length of Commitment

We estimated a need for 4 to 6 hours a week and asked for a minimum of a six-month commitment, since we would be sinking resources into this person through training and staff support.

Benefits of Volunteering

Reiterating the impact statement here reminds the potential volunteer that the person will be doing something important with his or her time. Another benefit is the opportunity to learn something that could also be used in another setting—paid or volunteer.

Our internal volunteer engagement team was able to get approval to change state library policy to provide a library card for volunteers (before that, cards were only available to state employees). And another great benefit was that this didn't have to be someone who actually came to the office to do all the work—it could be done virtually.

After interviews, we selected Kelley—someone who was passionately interested in volunteering and had a background in human resources. After a few months, she suggested that her job be increased to include scheduling the most qualified volunteers with an internal interview panel, and after the interviews, check volunteer references.

Later, when we added one of the available volunteer management systems—Volgistics—to our volunteer engagement toolbox, Kelley asked to be trained to use it and added to her workload the monthly data entry of volunteer hours. (More about volunteer management systems in Chapter 7, in section "Data Management.")

She opted to do some of her work from our office and some from home. She religiously attended our internal volunteer management team meetings, and we found her human resources expertise to be very helpful.

About two years into her service, she asked me for a reference, which I gladly gave, and she successfully acquired a part-time position as volunteer coordinator with a local organization. She continued volunteering with us, however, working our needs around her work schedule.

CHAPTER SUMMARY

The most important thing to know is that motivation comes from the volunteers themselves—motivation is not something you do to them. You must identify their individual reasons for volunteering—their motivation—and offer each a volunteer job that will satisfy his or her motivation, while meeting your needs at the same time.

The most important thing you'll do in your volunteer engagement efforts is designing volunteer job descriptions. This planning tool will help you succeed with all other aspects of the process. The job description is the basis for finding the right volunteer, and the key to keeping the good ones. And getting the right volunteer in the right job will go a long way to gaining staff buy-in for volunteer engagement. (For a look at more sample library volunteer job descriptions, visit the Get Involved Clearinghouse,[7] a searchable database of tools and practices that will help keep you from reinventing the wheel.)

So why don't people volunteer? PTO Today[8] cites these reasons:

- "What they do as a volunteer doesn't match what they had hoped to get out of volunteering.
- They don't clearly understand what they are being asked to do.
- They have an idealized view of people who volunteer and feel that they don't measure up.
- They tried, but no one contacted them. Or they showed up but were not needed or were not given anything meaningful to do.
- No one asked them."

NOTES

1. Ellis, Susan J., "Why Volunteer?" https://www.energizeinc.com/art/why-volunteer (accessed March 20, 2017).

2. Saxton, Joe, Tim Harrison, and Mhairi Guild, "The New Alchemy: How Volunteering Turns Donations of Time and Talent into Human Gold," 2015, p. 82. https://nfpsynergy.net/free-report/new-alchemy (accessed March 21, 2017).

3. LinkedIn for Good. https://linkedinforgood.linkedin.com/programs/linkedin-members (accessed October 19, 2017).

4. Fritz, Joanne, 2017, "15 Unexpected Benefits of Volunteering That Will Inspire You." https://www.thebalance.com/unexpected-benefits-of-volunteering-4132453 (accessed October 19, 2017).

5. United Health Care and VolunteerMatch, 2017, "Doing Good Is Good for You." https://newsroom.uhc.com/content/dam/newsroom/2017_VolunteerStudy_Summary_Web.pdf (accessed October 23, 2017).

6. The Monrovia Public Library's Volunteer Management Team produced two brief videos totaling about 7 minutes describing their work and sharing their strategies and tips. They are available for viewing at http://www.getinvolvedca.org/resource/training-materials/meet-volunteer-management-team-monrovia-public-library-part-1 and http://www.getinvolvedca.org/resource/training-materials/volunteer-management-team-tips-and-strategies-monrovia-public-library (accessed October 11, 2017).

7. Get Involved Clearinghouse, www.getinvolvedclearinghouse.org (accessed September 26, 2017).

8. Beck, Evelyn, "Why Don't People Volunteer?" 2015. https://www.ptotoday.com/pto-today-articles/article/5940-why-dont-people-volunteer (accessed March 22, 2017).

Volunteer Job Description: Public Speaker

LEHN PUBLIC LIBRARY

Position Overview and Impact: Make presentations about the library to community groups to raise awareness about what the library has to offer, and to attract potential library users, volunteers, and supporters.

Key Responsibilities:

1. Attend a 2-hour orientation to the library and on its public speaking objectives, presentation outline, and materials that have been prepared.
2. Respond to requests to speak based on your schedule when speaker's bureau coordinator contacts you with a speaking engagement.
3. Report data on number of attendees, particular interests of the group, and/or unanswered questions to the speaker's bureau coordinator within three days of speaking engagements.

Qualifications:

- Commitment to the library's vision and mission
- Successful public speaking experience

Training and Support Provided: Orientation to the library, and training on public speaking objectives, outline, and materials, as well as access to speaker's bureau coordinator as needed.

Time Commitment: Average 3–5 hours per month based on number of speaking engagements offered to you that fit into your schedule.

Length of Commitment: Minimum six-month commitment requested

Benefits of Volunteering:

- Assist the library in spreading the word to attract new users and supporters.
- Utilize skills in public speaking.
- Develop new community contacts.

Ongoing Library Contact: Speaker's Bureau Coordinator

Location: Aside from training and other meetings at the library, most of the work for this position will be done at the locations where community groups have requested a presentation.

Contact Person: Carla Lehn, Library Volunteer Coordinator (916) 555-7743 /clehn@library.ca.gov

Date Revised: 3/2017

Volunteer Job Description: Speaker's Bureau Coordinator

LEHN PUBLIC LIBRARY

Position Overview and Impact: Manage the library project that delivers presentations about the library to community groups to raise awareness about what the library has to offer, and to attract potential library users, volunteers, and supporters.

Key Responsibilities:

1. In conjunction with the library director, develop speaking engagement objectives and speaker presentation outline and materials.
2. Recruit, train, schedule, and oversee volunteer public speakers.
3. Identify priority community groups to contact for speaking engagements in conjunction with library director. Contact the groups and schedule a speaking engagement on their calendar.
4. Contact and schedule a trained volunteer speaker to attend each engagement.
5. Track and report volunteer hours and speaking engagement statistics quarterly.

Qualifications:

- Commitment to the Library vision and mission
- Successful public speaking experience and project management skills
- Good community contacts

Training and Support Provided: Orientation to the library and at least quarterly contact with the library director to plan activities, monitor progress, and provide problem-solving support.

Time Commitment: Average 8–10 hours per month from home around your schedule

Length of Commitment: Minimum one-year commitment requested

Benefits of Volunteering:

- Assist the library in spreading the word to attract new users and supporters.
- Utilize skills in program management, and gain skills in volunteer engagement.
- Utilize public speaking skills.
- Utilize current and develop new community contacts.

Ongoing Library Contact: Library Director

Location: Aside from meetings with the library director for planning purposes, much of this work can be done remotely.

Contact Person: Carla Lehn, Library Volunteer Coordinator (916) 555-7743 /clehn@library.ca.gov

Date Revised: 3/2017

Volunteer Job Description: Assistant Volunteer Coordinator

CALIFORNIA STATE LIBRARY

Position Overview and Impact: Supports the engagement of volunteers to assist in achieving the state library's information and cultural heritage mission, and increase the library's visibility and community connections.

Key Responsibilities:

1. Check the state library's VolunteerMatch account at least three times per week for new volunteers who have expressed interest.
2. Compare new applications with job description to identify qualified candidates. Share qualified candidate applications with appropriate staff member(s), and follow up to determine which, if any, they wish to interview.
3. As time allows, follow up with potential volunteers who did not submit an application to be sure they understood that was the next step.
4. If schedule permits, serve as a member of the internal volunteer engagement team (monthly).

Qualifications:

- Commitment to volunteerism and interest in learning about volunteer engagement practices.
- Good organizational skills and high level of comfort with online communication.
- Good written and oral communication skills.
- Ability to maintain confidentiality.
- Human resources experience helpful but not required.

On-Going Library Contact: Carla Lehn, Library Development Services

Training and Support Provided: Training on how to use VolunteerMatch and state library volunteer policies and procedures. Meetings with staff as needed for coordination and problem solving.

Time Commitment: 4–6 hours per week

Length of Commitment: Minimum six-month commitment requested

Benefits of Volunteering:

- Assist with extending the state library's reach into the community, and increase services to library users.
- Opportunity to learn about volunteer engagement practices.

- Work could be done at the library or virtually (from volunteer's computer and phone).

Initial Library Contact: Carla Lehn, **clehn@library.ca.gov/**916-555-1234

Date Revised: 3/2017

4

Volunteer Recruitment

Chapter 3 confirmed the importance of volunteer job descriptions. One of the biggest reasons for having them is that they focus recruitment strategy for each volunteer job. Good recruitment and placement can't be done without a clear and meaningful job description because it delineates the skills and qualifications required, the time commitment needed, and benefits the volunteer will derive.

Remember that you're looking to make a mutually beneficial exchange with all volunteers—they get something they want, and you get something you need. If you offer the same volunteer assignment to every potential volunteer without determining his or her motivation for volunteering in the first place, you will have many bad outcomes.

Some people will be perfectly happy with a shelving assignment; others would not find it to their liking. By the same token, not everyone can be a public relations volunteer, because not everyone has that expertise or interest.

If you're having a problem with volunteers not following through on commitments, or they drop out shortly after the training, that's a symptom that shows you're not paying close enough attention to your recruitment and placement practices. If volunteers don't have the qualifications required, or the assignment selected for them is not fulfilling their needs and interests, they will be uncomfortable in it, and will probably stop showing up. Placing the right person in an assignment from the beginning prevents a multitude of problems.

A SPECIAL WORD FOR FRIENDS OF THE LIBRARY ABOUT VOLUNTEER RECRUITMENT

Usually Friends groups just ask for "volunteers." This doesn't help today's volunteers, who want to know what volunteer positions are available, what skills are needed, and how much of their time it will take. Sally Gardner Reed says that the Friends' leadership should be "armed with the information they need to tell a potential volunteer exactly what he or she is being asked to do. Are they asking this person to design a brochure, work with the printer, or distribute the brochure to outside agencies? Now they are asking a potential volunteer to engage in one discrete task within an exact time frame."[1]

RECRUITMENT METHODS

Passive Recruitment

Many recruiters only use methods like posting "Volunteer Here" flyers in the library. Even if you have a volunteer page on your website, they have to find you. Both are passive recruitment methods. By using only passive approaches, your recruitment is limited to people who use the library. If one of the reasons you have elected to expand volunteer engagement is to increase your library's community engagement by cultivating volunteers who will eventually transform into library supporters and advocates, you're shooting yourself in the foot by using only passive volunteer recruitment methods.

Targeted Recruitment

Finding a potential volunteer with specific skills, like graphic design or event planning, won't happen if you just wait for one to walk through the door and respond to the "Volunteer Here" poster. Instead, use your carefully crafted job description like a heat-seeking missile to help you find the perfect person. Targeted recruitment is what this approach is called, and here's how to do it.

Using the Targeted Recruitment Plan (in the Appendix for this chapter) together with a copy of the volunteer job description, sit down with a couple others—staff, volunteers, Friends, or board members. It's not as effective if you try to do this alone, because there's so much more to build on if you have others to work with. Relying only on who and what *you* know will vastly limit your ability to find the people you need. Now, use the worksheet:

Qualifications and Benefits to the Volunteer

Review the qualifications and benefits in the job description again, and then ask yourselves, "Why would somebody, or some group, want this volunteer assignment? What's in it for them?"

How Could We Locate Them?

Now consider where you might find people with these qualifications. Could they be found in a group of some kind? Foster grandparent recruiters would probably begin at Senior Centers, right?

So, to find people with computer skills, you might start with organizations that sell or repair computers. There are also plenty of computer experts in colleges, high schools, and corporate IT departments. Could a local business provide that kind of support as part of their local community service commitment?

Service clubs can be tremendous sources of volunteers—Rotary and Elks, for example. Although they may have their own specific projects they're working on, they are sometimes looking for one to become involved with. If you're not a member, probably other staff members, volunteers, Friends, and board members are. You might want to consider joining a club both as a service to your community and to grow your own network.

Professional associations of accountants, nurses, public relations professionals, dentists, human resources managers—there's a professional association for almost anything—can be a gold mine for volunteer recruitment. Many are local chapters of national associations, and their members come together to network, access professional development opportunities, and lobby government on issues of interest to the profession. They are also often working on community service goals. Use that *Encyclopedia of Associations* in your Reference department to find a place to start looking for the skills you need.

The point is not to limit your options. Is there a project in the children's room that could be done by a couple or a family? Or might they adopt a shut-in from your book delivery program? The right volunteer position could provide a couple or family with real quality time together while providing an important service.

Maybe an organization could partner on a logical project—what about partnering with Meals on Wheels on homebound delivery? Could a couple of Scout troops rotate months to be responsible for a bulletin board or table display?

Personal Connections and the Best Person to Do the Asking

Now think about who you and your team know that either has the skills you're seeking, or knows someone who knows that type of person. Who among you knows someone that has a contact with that business or professional association? You're naming names at this point. The small group that's helping you with this exercise can expand the pool of possible contacts to help find the right person.

Selecting the person to do the asking is very important. Preferably, you select someone who knows the person being approached. The volunteer engagement coordinator is not necessarily always the best recruiter—there just might be someone better in a specific situation—perhaps the library director is a Chamber of Commerce member, or a board member's significant other is a bank manager, or one of your volunteers belongs to the local public relations association. The volunteer engagement coordinator can help him or her ask—the one who knows the person can set up the meeting, begin the conversation, and do the asking after you explain what's needed and answer questions.

I don't know who said it, but one of my favorite quotes is: "Luck is when opportunity meets preparation." Imagine the library director or Friends' president at their Lions luncheon, at a table with the director of a public relations firm. If they don't discuss your need for a graphic artist or a public relations plan with that person, a golden opportunity has been missed.

And if you haven't kept them updated on your volunteer recruitment needs, they can't even begin to have that discussion. Keep potential recruiters informed so that opportunities won't be missed.

People currently volunteering with you can be of great help in recruitment—they have lives outside the library, remember—but they can only help if they know what you're looking for. When people are asked by someone they already know and trust, they are much more likely to say yes.

REAL-LIFE EXAMPLE: PERSONAL CONNECTIONS AND THE BEST PERSON TO DO THE ASKING

Once a nonprofit agency had to file bankruptcy in our town because of a wrongful termination lawsuit, and many in our nonprofit community were on edge. I was asked to provide assistance to nonprofits on personnel law. I'm not a lawyer, so I knew I needed help. I reached out to a board member who was a professional human resources manager and explained the situation. She had a professional contact with a labor lawyer, and that person knew the chair of the County Bar Association, who knew others with that expertise.

My board member invited them to attend a single meeting so we could "pick their brains" on the subject. She opened with a brief explanation of the need, and before that 2-hour meeting was over, the lawyers at the table had created a 10-session training program on the subject, volunteering attorneys from their firms as trainers at no cost. All they wanted us to do was advertise the workshops among organizations in the community who could benefit.

They knew who the right people were to have at the table—people I didn't know—and then personally asked them to be involved. And, because of their knowledge of the subject, they were able to design an approach to address the need at a level that they were willing to participate.

LOCAL RECRUITMENT OPTIONS

In Chapter 2, Trend 6—"Collaborations with Other Organizations"—you'll find information on local volunteer support organizations like Volunteer Centers and HandsOn Networks—organizations that are in business to help with volunteer recruitment. Other local recruitment help may come from your local newspaper, United Way, or your city or county government. Be sure to locate those that are available in your area. Get to know them and how they can help.

ONLINE RECRUITMENT

In Chapter 2, Trend 5, online recruitment was briefly introduced, and a number of online recruitment sites were mentioned—some that even have a companion app for your phone.

You may have something on your library's website that gives people information about how to volunteer. Just remember that if it isn't easy to find, or doesn't give enough information or a way to sign up, it's a passive approach to recruitment.

If you haven't tried one of the online volunteer recruitment sites, you should. They extend your reach far beyond people you know—even to people who've never volunteered at a library before! If you have tried one, and felt you didn't get what you needed, I encourage you to try again—I'll share some tips below on how to make it work for you.

Before beginning, however, please note that it's not recommended that you exclusively use online recruitment to find volunteers. It should be considered one important tool in your recruitment toolbox, along with the others previously mentioned.

Online recruitment is a targeted recruitment approach because people who visit those sites are there because they are looking for a volunteer opportunity. They can search by city or by zip code, and select their favorites based on their interests and the skills they want to share.

ONLINE RECRUITMENT WITH VOLUNTEERMATCH.ORG

I'm sharing what I know about VolunteerMatch.org because I have the most experience with it, but you'll find instructions, resources, toolkits, and online support information on the other platforms' websites, as well as on VolunteerMatch.org (see Figure 4.1).

More than 110,000 organizations across the country use VolunteerMatch in their search for volunteers, and more than 15 million unique visitors annually come to the site to find a volunteer opportunity. LinkedIn shares appropriate skilled volunteer opportunities to another 10 million professionals

FIGURE 4.1. VolunteerMatch Home Page

through a partnership with VolunteerMatch, and more than 3.2 million employees see your volunteer opportunities either via a web-based solution a company uses that was built by VolunteerMatch, or through partnerships with several corporate giving platforms, like Bright Funds, Causecast, and YourCause.

Any organization seeking volunteers can create a free account on VolunteerMatch and begin posting volunteer opportunities. When a volunteer types in his or her zip code, the site returns a list of opportunities within a 20-mile radius, in order of those posted most recently. When a volunteer finds one that looks interesting, he or she clicks the "I Want to Help" button, which generates an e-mail message with the volunteer's contact information directly to whoever in your organization you told it to go to—the volunteer coordinator if you have one, or the staff person who will work directly with this volunteer. You decide based on your internal structure and needs. Then you follow up with the volunteer to get the discussion started.

Here are some tips for getting the most out of using VolunteerMatch.org:

- Although advanced search options are available, many searches are based solely on location. You'll also notice on the search page that tabs are available for the volunteer to look at "Local" or "Virtual" options to volunteer.
- Your volunteer opportunity will need to stand out from the crowd because in the list that's returned, they all look basically the same. Three strategies can help it stand out:
  1. An engaging "action" title, that states, or at least hints at the outcome—what difference it will make if they choose to volunteer in this position?

For example, if you seek volunteer tutors for your English as a Second Language (ESL) program, don't just give it the title "Tutor," or "Volunteer Tutor." Consider something like "Change a Life: Help an Adult Learn English."

2. Ask your volunteers to "Review" the job they're doing for you on VolunteerMatch. When they do, orange stars will appear on your posting that direct the eye's attention to it.
3. Keep your posting at the top of the list, rather than having it get pushed down by new opportunities being posted by other organizations in your zip code. (Note: "Reposting" is the strategy for this—it is available as one of a number of VolunteerMatch Premium tools if you purchase a Premium account instead of just the free one. At this writing the Premium account fee is $9.95 per month or $99 per year.[2] (More about Premium tools both in end note 2 and later in this chapter.)

- A good posting includes a photo. But don't just use a picture of your library or your logo; use a photo that shows what it looks like to do this volunteer job—so the potential volunteers can see themselves doing it.[3]
- While you want to give potential volunteers enough information to excite them about your volunteer position, you'll want to use only about 100 words taken from your prepared job description. Try to answer as many of their initial questions as you can in the posting: What will I be doing? How much time does it take? Are there any special qualifications or skills I need to have?
- Be sure to check your spelling and grammar! VolunteerMatch had a volunteer research the opportunities that got the most and the least hits—the one thing all the fewest hit postings had in common was poor grammar and/or misspelled words.
- Another great feature is the ability to share your posting via e-mail or directly to Facebook, Twitter, and LinkedIn. Post it to your library's social media accounts, then staff, volunteers, Friends of the Library, and your board members can share with their networks, expanding your reach dramatically.
- You should be aware that volunteers are often "shopping" for the right opportunity on VolunteerMatch and may have clicked on the "I Want to Help" button for a number of options to learn more about them before making a decision about which one is right for them. Getting in touch right away gives you first crack over the others they chose and will help them decide. If they're not interested after all, this helps to weed them out quickly.

Here's a quick overview of just a few of the additional VolunteerMatch tools that come with a Premium (paid) account[4]:

Reposting: As mentioned earlier, the search default brings up volunteer opportunities by the most recent date they were posted. With this feature, you can repost an opportunity to the top of the search with just one click. Try it a few times and then check back to see how long you can wait before reposting again to keep it at the top.[5]

Customize the connection e-mail volunteers receive. Rather than just having the volunteers receive the generic reply from VolunteerMatch saying they will notify the organization of their interest, you can customize the automatic response to give them additional information, including attaching documents like a full job description, training information, or your volunteer application. You can even provide a link to your own online application to help them get started. (*Note:* If you don't have an online application yet, be sure to review volunteer management systems in Chapter 7, as some of them provide that option for you.)

Recruit volunteers on your website using Promote Your Listings. By using the Promote Your Listings tool you can create your volunteer opportunity once on VolunteerMatch and then easily display it in multiple places on your website, such as the home page, blog, or volunteering section.[6]

Volunteers who come to you through VolunteerMatch can be taken through your regular on-boarding process—application, interview, background check, etc.—just like you would with a volunteer recruited another way.

You should be aware that on average about 25 percent of the potential volunteers who click on the "I Want to Help" button will actually become volunteers for you. This is because they are shopping for the right opportunity and may be looking at several. You only want the ones that are a good fit, anyway, so expect some to weed themselves out during this process.

INEFFECTIVE RECRUITMENT STRATEGIES

Here are a few recruitment "cautions":

- **Don't use only one recruitment method.** Implement a repertoire of methods that will create a pool of potential volunteers with the skills you require.
- **Don't use guilt or coercion.** People who feel roped into volunteering won't stay.
- **Don't do recruitment all by yourself.** Use the Targeted Recruitment Plan in the Appendix and get a few others together to add their ideas and networks to the mix.
- **Don't underestimate the job.** Describe it honestly—what's required and how long it will take—then hold out for the right person.
- **Don't settle.** What you're doing is important. You want the best volunteer for the job—the one who meets your needs and qualifications, so you can provide the highest level of service.[7]
- **Don't make assumptions.** One human resources professional may want to volunteer his or her skills, while another might want to get away from human resources and shelve books instead.
- **You are not required to say yes to every person who wants to volunteer.** Having a good volunteer job description helps people without the right

qualifications or motivations screen themselves out. Or once in a conversation about the position, and you find it's not a good fit, you can say: "You know, I just don't think I have something that suits you right now. I wouldn't want you to come here and be unhappy. Would you like me to call the Volunteer Center for you? They take requests for volunteers from many organizations in the community." Or "Let me show you how to use VolunteerMatch, where lots of local organizations post their volunteer opportunities."

WHAT IF THEY SAY NO?

Make sure to provide an opportunity for the volunteer to say no. Don't force the volunteer to take the assignment if it's not a good fit. Anyway, you *want* the person to say no if the assignment doesn't fit with his or her skills, interests, or availability.

Remember this: *It's always better to have a vacancy than to have the wrong volunteer in the position.* Use that job description with the volunteer to be sure you both have a clear understanding of the job. Selecting the wrong person creates the volunteer equivalent of a personnel problem, causing you to spend time coaching and retraining, transferring, or even firing a volunteer.

You can avoid all that by doing careful screening and selection. Put someone in the right job to begin with, and everyone will be happier.

CHAPTER SUMMARY

Your carefully designed volunteer job descriptions will help with all aspects of the recruitment process. They will help to identify what skills are needed for the position, which will assist with your use of the Targeted Recruitment Plan to find the right person for the right job. Employing multiple recruitment methods will expand your reach beyond library patrons and those you already know. Adding one or more online recruitment options might even attract people who haven't been in the library for a long time, but were interested in the volunteer opportunity you posted there that meets their skills and interests.

NOTES

1. Reed, Sally Gardner, *The Good, the Great, and the Unfriendly: A Librarian's Guide to Working with Friends Groups* (Chicago: American Library Association, 2017).

2. Find a comparison of features available in VolunteerMatch Basic (free) accounts and Premium $9.95/month or $99/year. https://www.volunteermatch.org/nonprofits (accessed March 26, 2017).

3. The Get Involved Clearinghouse is a searchable online database of resources for library volunteer engagement programs. It includes management tools such as volunteer engagement policies and handbooks, sample volunteer job descriptions,

training materials that can be downloaded and used or revised for your use, and photos that have been sized to be posted on VolunteerMatch.org. Originally designed as part of California's Get Involved: Powered by Your Library initiative, the Clearinghouse was expanded in 2017 through a grant to a collaborative of four state library agencies—Arizona, California, Idaho, and Texas—from the Institute for Museum and Library Services' Laura Bush 21st Century Librarian Program. www.getinvolvedclearinghouse.org (accessed March 31, 2017).

4. VolunteerMatch, "Upgrading and Using Premium Tools." https://vmhelp.zendesk.com/hc/en-us/sections/202853417-Upgrading-Using-Premium-Tools (accessed March 26, 2017).

5. A 2.5-minute video on how to Repost can be found here: http://www.getinvolvedca.org/resource/training-materials/getting-highest-visibility-volunteermatch-how-repost-your-listing (accessed September 26, 2017).

6. View library websites using Promote your Listings here: http://www.huntingtonbeachca.gov/government/departments/library/volunteers or http://www.cityoflivermore.net/citygov/lib/howdoi/volunteer/default.htm—clicking on the title of the volunteer job takes you right to the opportunity posted on VolunteerMatch (accessed March 31, 2017).

7. If you would like to hear Lily, a library literacy specialist, talking about "raising the bar" in her volunteer recruitment, take a look at this 90-second video clip: http://www.youtube.com/watch?v=rxqvP6xhO1Q (accessed March 26, 2017).

Targeted Recruitment Plan

Volunteer Position: ______________________________

From the Volunteer Position Description:

What qualifications must this person have?	**What benefits will the volunteer receive?**
(skills, attitudes, experience, time required)	(share skills, meet people, gain skills/experience)

How Could We Locate Them?

Who has these qualifications?	**Do people like these congregate anywhere?**
(a particular profession, age range, educational level, etc.)	(professional association, service club, corporate volunteer program, faith community?)

Personal Connections	Local Recruitment Options	Online Recruitment Resource
Who do we know who knows people like this? Who is the best person to ask?	**What local volunteer recruitment options do we have?**	**What online recruitment options do we have?**
(board member, current volunteer, professional in the field, spouse?)	(Volunteer Center, HandsOn Network, United Way, local newspaper, city or county government?)	(Volunteermatch.org, HandsOn Network, DoSomething.org, Serve.gov, etc.)

5

Success Factors for Volunteer Engagement

Lots of research exists on volunteerism, as well as many publications aimed at the profession of volunteer engagement. There is also access to information and support from local, national, and international professional associations. From both research and experience, it's clear that there are specific factors required to achieve success with volunteer engagement.

1. Meaningful written volunteer position descriptions
2. Targeted recruitment
3. Careful screening
4. Orientation and training
5. Staff buy-in
6. Collaboration, support, and feedback
7. Recognition/acknowledgment
8. Sustainability strategies

In designing your volunteer engagement initiative, you must ensure that someone has responsibility for each of these. The optimum structure includes a paid volunteer coordinator, but not everyone has that capability just yet. To be successful, however, requires identifying someone to be responsible for these factors. You'll find more on staffing for volunteer engagement in Chapter 6, "How It All Gets Done."

Meaningful written job descriptions were covered in depth in Chapter 3, and targeted recruitment in Chapter 4. The remaining success factors are described below.

SUCCESS FACTOR 3: CAREFUL SCREENING

Often people think of volunteer screening as just criminal history background checks. Although that may be one of the screening steps your library takes for some or all volunteer positions, background checks alone do not constitute careful screening. You'll find more on background checks in Chapter 7, "Administrative and Legal Issues."

Screening volunteers is the process of determining if they are the right match for the job—if they have the right qualifications; if their skill level is high enough to meet your needs; if their schedule will accommodate the work; and if so, does the job interest them?

The first screening step is when the volunteer reviews the job description you've carefully developed, and decides whether or not it looks like something he or she is interested in. This might happen on your website, on VolunteerMatch, or another online recruitment platform—when the volunteer reviews the job and either calls, e-mails, or clicks to demonstrate interest. Reviewing the job description for the first time might also happen when you provide it after an initial phone call or in a first meeting with the volunteer.

Interviewing

A key part of volunteer screening is the interview. Sometimes people think that interviewing volunteers seems like overkill—it takes too much time and sounds too formal for volunteer work. On the contrary! The volunteers want to clearly understand what's being asked before taking the job, and they want to know they can be successful. Interviewing also shows that you're serious about this position and want to be sure you have just the right people.

The job description is also used in the interview to discuss qualifications for the position, as well as job duties, and the time commitment required. A good conversation will help both you and the volunteer make an informed decision about whether or not they are both motivated by and qualified for this opportunity.

If they determine it's not of interest, you hopefully have other job descriptions to share. If you don't have other opportunities, be prepared to refer them to your local volunteer center or one of the online recruitment search engines.

You can watch a library staff member talk about how volunteer engagement has changed as the result of the addition of interviews to the process in a short video clip.[1]

Seek more guidance about interviewing from human resources personnel. If your library itself doesn't have access to someone like that, and you're not part of a city or county that does, consider finding a local or virtual volunteer with those skills and experience to help guide your understanding of what is appropriate.

The California State Library's volunteer engagement team received terrific guidance from the human resources director:

- Have a team of two or three people on each interview panel. Have the same panel interview every volunteer seeking the same position.
- Include on the panel at least one staff member who will be working with this volunteer position.

These suggestions ensure fairness for the volunteers and encourage ownership of the successful candidate(s) by the staff who will be working most closely with them. The human resources staff agreed to review our interview questions for each position in advance, which was also very helpful.

Because you'll be looking for different skills and capabilities, the interview questions for each position will be different. Discuss responsibilities and qualifications for the job, why they think they would be a good fit for it, and what they might like to gain from volunteering at the library. You will also want to ask questions that help to assess particular skills and strengths critical to the position (see Table 5.1).

Behavior-based interviewing assumes that the best predictor of future behavior is past behavior. Elisa Kosarin[2] says that her volunteer retention

TABLE 5.1. Types of Interview Questions

What You're Looking For	Sample Questions
Background	Tell me a little about yourself. Do you have any previous volunteer experiences? Tell me about them.
Interest in the position	What interests you about this position? What do you hope to gain for yourself by volunteering at the library?
Problem-solving ability	What ideas do you have for helping the library reach more people who would benefit from our home delivery program?
Experience with a critical task	Describe a time where you were tasked with leading a team. What went well? What didn't? What might you do differently next time?
Skills	Tell us about your experience managing social media accounts. What have been your greatest successes? (For this job or others such as writing, photography, brochure or web design, etc., ask the volunteer in advance to be ready to show samples of his or her work in the interview.)
Handling difficult situations	You are in charge of a large event, and two hours before it's to begin, you learn that two key volunteers won't be able to make it. What steps would you take to resolve this situation?

increased dramatically using this method. "You ask questions that require your applicants to give examples of the competencies you seek. Questions usually begin one of two ways: 'Tell me about a time when . . .' or 'Give me an example of. . . .'" She suggests beginning by identifying the competencies required to be successful in the position—found in the responsibilities and qualifications in the volunteer job description—and then crafting questions that encourage the applicant to tell a story that will give you insights into the person's past behavior in that area.

Reference Checks

Whether you are interviewing volunteer applicants with a particular skill set required for the position, or just need recruits who have a good work ethic and are dependable and trustworthy, checking references after the interview will help you complete the picture and make the best decision. If the skill set is something that can be shown to you, like graphic design, writing, or newsletter production, be sure to ask the applicants to be prepared to show you examples of their work in the interview.

You can ask for references on the volunteer application, or if you plan to ask for them during the interview, be sure to let the interviewee know in advance so he or she can be prepared. Here's one way to ask: "Please list the names, e-mails, and phone numbers of two individuals we may contact as a reference. Do not list relatives. At least one should be of a professional nature (a work or volunteer supervisor, teacher, etc.)."

At the end of the interview, you can tell the candidate that once all the interviews are completed, you'll be checking references and will be in touch once a decision is made.

I sometimes get so excited about a candidate during an interview that I want to reach across the desk and sign the person right up. That's not the best approach. Finish all the candidate interviews and confer with your team before offering the position to someone. Besides you and your team needing to process what you've heard and completing the reference checks, you want the candidate to have time to reflect on what he or she learned in the interview before being asked to make a decision.

Once the interview team makes the decision, call the person you've selected, and be sure to ask these questions suggested from Katie Zwetzig[3]:

- What questions have come up since we last spoke?
- What were your "aha" moments from our interview?
- What else has occurred to you over the past few days? Great ideas? Concerns?

These questions are designed to give them the opportunity to opt out if they want to. You don't want someone accepting who doesn't truly want to be there, after all."

If they accept your offer, schedule a first meeting within a week or so to get started.

Saying No to a Volunteer after the Interview

When interviewing several people for a position that requires only one volunteer, you'll need to be prepared to say no to the candidates you don't choose. Explain that your team "selected another candidate whose experience and qualifications most closely fit our needs." If you have other positions available that you think the volunteer would be a good fit for, describe them and offer to send the job description if they seem interested.

If you have nothing available, say so, and refer them to your local Volunteer Center or another organization in town if you know they might have something of interest, or at least to VolunteerMatch.org or another online recruitment site.

If you find that a volunteer is not a good fit for the job you've interviewed him or her for, explain as above that you selected a candidate that better met your needs. If you think the volunteer would be a good fit for another position you have available, mention it and ask if the person would like to take a look at the full job description. Otherwise, refer the applicant out as described above.

If you find that a volunteer is not a good fit for the job you've interviewed them for, and you don't want to pursue engaging them any further, again, explain as above that you selected a candidate that better met your needs, and that you don't have another position that would be a good fit. Because you want them to be happy, and to share their interest in volunteering in the community, offer them information about the local Volunteer Center, and/or an online recruitment site. In a 2017 article, Elisa Kosarin[4] suggests that you "Frame the conversation from the applicant's point of view: Explain that, from your experience, the applicant will feel frustrated or unfulfilled in this position rather than rewarded."

Selecting the right volunteer for the right job is one of the most critical tasks of the volunteer engagement coordinator and interview team. Putting the wrong volunteer in a position creates a headache for you and for the staff and volunteers the person will be working with, which can lead to staff resistance to volunteer engagement. Gaining or maintaining staff buy-in is a continuous process, and picking the volunteers whose skills and interests most match those of the job description that's been created is a critical part of the process.

In Chapter 4, when discussing what happens if the potential volunteer says no during recruitment, I suggested that a vacancy is preferable to having the wrong volunteer. Selecting the wrong person will likely create a personnel problem. Instead of just having a vacancy, you'll find yourself spending time coaching and retraining, transferring, or even firing a volunteer.

Kosarin[5] further notes: "Turning away volunteers is never fun. But turning away unqualified volunteers is the flip side of the management coin. It's a signal that you are clear on who works for your program and who doesn't. It means you see how an unqualified volunteer strains capacity when you are committed to keeping your program strong."

Placement Considerations

Remember that just because you're interviewing attorneys, doesn't mean they are looking to share their legal skills. Some will want to do that and others won't. Some might be looking for an escape from their profession in their volunteer work. And don't assume that if they live far away they're not a good fit. The commute may be worth it to them to get the experience offered by the position. Be sure to ask about those things in the interview to allow the candidates to give you a complete picture of what they are or are not willing to do.

What if the volunteer you just interviewed is perfect for one part of the job but not for another? Could you get those things the volunteer is not suited for done in another way? Perhaps you could break the job into smaller pieces and recruit for a different volunteer(s) to cover those. Just be careful not to reduce the job responsibilities for this volunteer unless the person is worth it for some reason, and you've devised another way to get the rest done.

You might discover a volunteer has a particular skill that you'd love to be able to take advantage of, but you don't have a written job description for it. Briefly discuss what you have in mind with the volunteer, and if he or she is interested, write up a job description and share it with the applicant for more discussion before finalizing the person's engagement.

REAL-LIFE EXAMPLE: SOCIAL MEDIA SPECIALIST, NO—PHOTOGRAPHER, YES

One of the candidates we interviewed for the social media specialist volunteer position was a young woman just out of college looking for a way to help while she completed her job search. During the interview, she mentioned that she had taken a look at our social media offerings, found that we didn't use Instagram, and asked why. I explained that we didn't have a lot of good photos to share—that when I asked libraries to provide photos of volunteers, they usually provided pictures of two people shaking hands holding up a certificate. Boring. What I wanted was good pictures of volunteers in action, but I couldn't seem to get those.

The interviewee showed us her Instagram account with some of the beautiful and creative photos she had taken and said she would be happy to help us with her photography skills as well. We briefly discussed the idea of arranging some library "photo shoots" so she could take pictures of volunteers in action and get signed release forms from her subjects while she was there. She liked the idea, so I designed a job description and sent it to her later for review. After a few minor mutually acceptable tweaks—like helping her with mileage reimbursement if I sent her far from home—we met again to finalize our agreement.

Although she didn't have as much social media management experience as we needed, she was a great "find" for a skill we hadn't yet considered—photography!

SUCCESS FACTOR 4: ORIENTATION AND TRAINING

Volunteers deserve both orientation and training. Here's the distinction between them:

Orientation

Providing an orientation session helps volunteers get the big picture—answering questions like: What's the mission of the organization? How do volunteers fit in? Be sure to provide everyone with an orientation—either in a group or individually.

But, please don't distribute written materials as a substitute for the orientation conversation. You hope and expect that they'll read it, but most often they won't. It's fine to distribute the *Volunteer Handbook* for them to review later, but it shouldn't take the place of a discussion and giving people an opportunity to ask questions.

As your program grows, you can even write position descriptions for volunteer trainers to deliver the orientations and free staff time from this task. You may also want to consider recruiting some skilled trainers who could help with designing the orientation. They may even be willing to present it to groups of new and/or potential volunteers, or possibly to train other staff or volunteers to make the presentation. As a place to begin, a suggested Volunteer Orientation and Training Outline is included in the Appendices for this chapter.

REAL-LIFE EXAMPLE: IMPORTANCE OF VOLUNTEER ORIENTATION

While working with a library on their volunteer engagement program, we asked a group of very experienced library volunteers to sit in on the newly designed volunteer orientation in order to provide feedback on how we could make it better for new volunteers. Shockingly, more than one of these longtime library volunteers wrote on their evaluation form: "Thank you for telling me about confidentiality at the library. I had never heard about that before. . . ." We assume too often that people know about the library's mission and practices. Hopefully, this example helps you see the importance of orienting volunteers to the library.

Training

In addition to an orientation, you'll need to provide job specific training for volunteers to carry out their responsibilities effectively. Volunteers assigned to jobs like book mending and adult literacy tutoring will need to be taught how to do the job. Volunteers assigned to the computer lab may not have to be trained on how to use a computer, but they need to know about any policies and procedures related to your lab, how the computer reservation system works, what data you want them to collect on their interactions, etc.

Training may take place one-on-one or in a group setting. You might also consider having a new volunteer "shadow" an experienced volunteer or mentor as part of the training.

Another consideration is to engage staff associated with the volunteer position in helping to design the training for it. Staff will want to be sure that volunteers have the information they need to do the job right. Asking for staff input on what should be included in the training can help allay their fears about volunteers' ability to do the job and help gain staff buy-in for volunteer engagement.

If staff members have the interest and time, inviting them to help with presentation of the training goes a long way to assure them that volunteers will be prepared to get the job done right, while rewarding interested staff members with an opportunity to learn or practice public speaking skills. Don't force staff involvement with presenting training if they are not interested—for many, fear of public speaking is second only to their fear of death!

Sometimes there won't be a need for skills training. For example, if you've been successful in finding an experienced public relations firm to create your annual report, they won't need training in annual report design. They should, however, get a thorough orientation to the library to be sure they clearly understand the library's philosophy and policy. They will also require a staff contact person to consult as they prepare this important document for the library. They'll also need to know from the outset what resources are or are not available for the project. For example, if they design a four-color annual report, and you have a one-color budget, you have just wasted their time, and they will not be happy as a result. (See more about this concept later in this chapter in "Collaborating with and Supporting Skilled Volunteers.")

In-Service Training

As policies, procedures, or equipment change, in-service training should be provided to volunteers.

If proposed budget cuts for the library have been proposed, be sure to keep volunteers informed, because their community connections perceive them to be library representatives and they will be asked about it. They deserve to be prepared with the basic information as well as where they can get specific questions answered if needed. And don't forget to tell them how they can help, because volunteers make terrific advocates!

Depending on what the changes or issues are, you can provide in-service training in a variety of ways: an in-person or online meeting, an e-mail blast, or individual updates provided by staff or experienced volunteers. If it's a budget or other community-level issue about the library, start with an e-mail blast including basic information, but also offer in-person or online meetings—preferably with the library director and/or board members in attendance—so there is an opportunity for questions. An online meeting can be recorded, and an in-person meeting can be videotaped. Links can then be posted for those who were unable to attend in real time.

Staff Training

Sometimes staff aren't ready to welcome volunteers with open arms. If they have received no training about working with volunteers or have had a bad volunteer experience in their past, they may not be ready to welcome volunteers into the fold.

Staff need the opportunity to understand why the library thinks it's important to utilize volunteers, and have a chance to ask questions and share concerns. (Are they trying to eliminate my job? . . .)

They also need to be clued in to volunteer engagement practices, as well as training in delegation and supervision skills. Feel free to use the materials in this book to craft training pieces for your staff.

SUCCESS FACTOR 5: STAFF BUY-IN

For many library staff the concept of engaging high-skilled volunteers is new. It takes time, communication, training, and some success in your library to overcome some staff's view that volunteers are more trouble than they're worth.

Even if you have found just the right volunteers, who have been carefully recruited, thoroughly screened, and given the perfect assignment both for the volunteers and for the library—if the volunteers pick up on the fact that staff don't feel good about them being there, they will feel uncomfortable, and won't stay.

Staff could resist volunteer engagement for any number of reasons. Their primary concern is often the fear being replaced by volunteers and losing their jobs—which is of course not the goal. The goal is to enhance or expand library services or capacity. But staff's concern that volunteers will replace them makes it important to have clear policies about *supplementing* not supplanting staff roles with volunteers. (See "Developing a Volunteer Engagement Mission Statement" section and Appendices in Chapter 1.)

Some staff have had a previous bad experience—they were assigned volunteers who were not selected or trained well enough, and many times, the staff were given little or no preparation for their role in volunteer engagement.

Changing the culture about volunteerism in general and about engaging high-skilled volunteers in particular will require some strategic steps on your part:

1. Ensure that the library director speaks at staff meetings about the fact that volunteer engagement is an important strategy for the library—a way to engage new library supporters and advocates. Including volunteer engagement in the library's strategic plan will also help to emphasize its importance with the staff.
2. Approach the staff "champions" first. These are the staff who "get it" and want to get started on some ideas for volunteer engagement they have. It's not necessary to implement this new strategy immediately throughout the whole library—start small. Try even just one skilled position, and when you share the first successes, other staff will be drawn to the idea.
3. Be a role model by engaging skilled volunteers in <u>your</u> office. It's hard to expect others to get on board if you're not willing to do it yourself.
4. Share with staff the goals and plans you have—how you're going to avoid problems by selecting the right volunteers and training them. Explain that if it doesn't work out, you'll be available to help. Engage the staff in helping design volunteer job descriptions and training materials for positions they will be working with—include them in volunteer interviews and even in doing some of the training themselves.

Staff resistance can be lowered by using some preventive measures. In Table 5.2, you'll find typical reasons why staff aren't supportive of volunteer engagement in the left column. Strategies for avoiding problems are in the middle, and the right column specifies where to find more assistance and examples in this book.

TABLE 5.2. Strategies for Encouraging Staff Buy-In

Reasons for Staff Concerns about Engaging Volunteers	Steps You Can Take to Avoid Problems	Where You Can Find Help in This Book
Fear of job replacement	Establish official policy on supplementing not supplanting staff positions.	Chapter 1, Mission Statements
	Clearly define roles, involve staff in that process.	Chapter 3, Job Descriptions
	Engage the union in volunteer engagement planning.	Chapter 1, Union Issues
Fear of decrease in quality or loss of control	Start small—"pilot" volunteer engagement with one or more staff "champions"—don't try to implement everywhere all at once.	Chapter 5, Staff Buy-In
	Involve staff in designing and presenting volunteer training.	Chapter 5, Training
	Train staff to be leaders and mentors.	Chapter 5, Training
Unclear about volunteer/staff roles	Provide written job descriptions and training for volunteers.	Chapter 3, Job Descriptions Chapter 5, Training
	Develop agreements between staff and volunteers.	Use the job description as an agreement and/or see Chapter 5, section "Collaborating with and Supporting Skilled Volunteers"
Previous bad experience with volunteers	Identify what's in it for the library.	Chapter 1, "Why Volunteers?"
	Show job description format and ask for staff help in writing some.	Chapter 3, Job Descriptions
	Train staff in volunteer engagement practices and delegation.	Chapter 5, Staff Training
	Reassure about careful screening, training, and ability to reassign or terminate volunteers if necessary.	Chapter 5, Screening, Training Chapter 5, Feedback

(continued)

TABLE 5.2. Strategies for Encouraging Staff Buy-In (*continued*)

Reasons for Staff Concerns about Engaging Volunteers	Steps You Can Take to Avoid Problems	Where You Can Find Help in This Book
	Include staff in volunteer interviews.	Chapter 5, Interviewing
	Offer your support.	Chapter 6, "How It All Gets Done"
Resent additional workload	Share stories of staff successes with volunteers.	Chapter 6, "How It All Gets Done"
	Redistribute workload if necessary.	
Believe there are things that volunteers shouldn't do in the library	Engage the library director and union representative in planning for volunteer engagement.	Chapter 6, "How It All Gets Done"
Fear of change	Management plays a visible and positive role in explaining the importance to the library.	Chapter 6, "How It All Gets Done"
	Create a volunteer engagement team to involve staff at all levels in planning for volunteer engagement.	Chapter 1, Mission Statements
	Identify internal "champions" to implement some examples—share success stories.	Chapter 5, Staff Buy-In
	Demonstrate your commitment to the concept by engaging volunteers in your work.	Chapter 5, Staff Buy-In

SUCCESS FACTOR 6: FEEDBACK, COLLABORATION, AND SUPPORT

Feedback

At the very least, make every volunteer feel welcome, and make sure they know who their "staff collaborator" is, so they know who they can approach with their questions and who to contact if they're sick or going out of town.

Occasionally volunteers may require some feedback on their work. Begin that conversation by just asking how they're doing. Often, they know they're having a problem, and will share their question or frustration right then. If not, mention one aspect of their work that you think is going well, and then suggest that you might want to talk again about this other aspect of the job. Start your conversation with the job description to determine what needs to be fixed. They may just need a bit more training or coaching to be sure everything is clear.

A library staff member once confided that she just couldn't bring herself to tell one volunteer that she was doing the assignment completely wrong, so she—the staff member—stayed after work, to redo the volunteer's assignment! Please don't do that!

If the volunteer's work is not accurate, you must be fair and tell the person. Others will know—or find out—if a volunteer isn't performing well, so don't embarrass that person by not intervening. Other volunteers and staff will wonder why you're not working to solve the problem. Letting a problem continue demeans the volunteers who are doing the job well and sends the message to staff that you weren't serious when you said that engaging volunteers wouldn't have an impact on the quality of the work.

Volunteers want to know if they're doing something wrong, and they want guidance on how to improve things. They volunteered in order to help, not to create work for you!

Sitting down for a periodic chat or at least asking volunteers to complete an annual self-assessment is important. This also provides an opportunity to see how they think it's going, as well as to get their feedback and ideas for improvement.

If coaching and retraining don't fix the problem, consider placing the volunteer in another position where the person can be successful. But don't hesitate to act if there's a serious problem—if a volunteer breaks confidentiality or safety rules, misrepresents the library, or is inappropriate with a patron, for example, you must address it right away. This is another place you will most definitely want guidance from a human resource professional, but yes, volunteers can be fired if their continued involvement will have a negative impact on the library. You'll find more on this in the "Can I Fire a Volunteer?" section of the Troubleshooting Appendix.

Collaborating with and Supporting Skilled Volunteers

High-skilled volunteers want collaboration, not supervision. Both you and they will want to connect regularly to ensure things are going as planned. In your first meeting after the interview, you'll be orienting the skilled volunteer to the organization and to any policies, procedures, or organizational norms the volunteer will need to be aware of to be effective in the job. If the person needs equipment or materials to complete the task, be sure he or she knows what the limits are and how to access them. Establish a timeline for completing the work, including how often you'll be meeting to check in on progress, and be sure the volunteer knows about any constraints on the project, such as budget or staff time. Then type up what was discussed and send it to the volunteer as your agreement.

REAL-LIFE EXAMPLE: DEVELOPING AN AGREEMENT WITH A SKILLED VOLUNTEER

The job description for the real-life public relations specialist volunteer mentioned in Chapter 2 is in the Appendices for this chapter. What he brought to the table was his many years of experience in planning public relations campaigns. What he needed was an understanding of the organization and guidelines for our work together.

In our first meeting after the interview, I oriented him to the state library and to the statewide adult literacy program. I shared, for example, that we didn't use the word "illiterate" to describe the people our libraries were serving, but instead talked about "low literate adults." I outlined our budget restrictions for the project, and together we worked back from the deadline date for the project to create a timeline for what would happen when and who was responsible.

We also established a regular Friday, 3:00 p.m. phone call to check in. If we had no need to meet on a particular Friday, we canceled via e-mail and during those strategy calls scheduled any other tasks or meetings required.

His role was to bring the skill, and mine was to support him in using it on behalf of the library. After our first meeting, he basically became a virtual volunteer. We met in person only when the situation required it, such as at strategy meetings with the state librarian.

SUCCESS FACTOR 7: RECOGNITION/ ACKNOWLEDGMENT

Although not a lot of research has been done on this topic, a 2013 study by Volunteer Canada[6] produced some interesting results. Their key findings showed that there were two top ways volunteers would like to be recognized: 80 percent said they would like to hear about how their work has made a difference, and nearly 70 percent said they would like to be thanked in person on an ongoing, informal basis.

Interestingly, the study found that volunteers' least preferred way to be recognized were banquets, formal gatherings, and public acknowledgment, even though those methods are commonly used by organizations as recognition strategies.

Libraries typically thank their volunteers with an event—a brunch, potluck, or reception that includes food, a thank you gift, such as a certificate, a 10-year pin, or a book bag, along with speeches from dignitaries like the library director or a city council member. If you're doing this too, just make sure it's working. If only a percentage of your volunteers are attending the event, how are the rest being thanked?

REAL-LIFE EXAMPLE: "CAREER PATH" AS RECOGNITION/ACKNOWLEDGMENT

Over the shame of a failed recognition event—nobody showed up!—we surveyed the volunteers asking how they would like to be recognized. The responses from volunteer trainers were very clear. The reason they volunteered to serve as a trainer was to get the chance to do more training, and the way they wanted to be recognized was to learn more about training techniques and getting a chance to present more often.

In response to this feedback, we started holding in-services periodically, so volunteers could learn a new training technique or watch other volunteers present a particularly effective exercise they had developed for use in their presentations. While meeting their desire to gain new training skills, we also made way for informal recognition—like the flip chart marker "corsages" we made, or the plastic safari hat given for handling a difficult assignment.

We started recognizing outstanding performance by giving volunteers the opportunity to learn and present a second topic, thus responding to their interest in getting to do more training. Interestingly this also met the need for more trainers in some topic areas—prior to that we thought we had to constantly recruit more new trainers to meet the demand. What we learned was that our current trainers wanted to do more!

The position of "lead trainer" for each topic was also established. Included in that job description was "mentoring" newer trainers for quality control purposes and maintaining contact with volunteers in their topic group when growth in the program and number of trainers began to exceed the ability of staff to maintain regular contact with every individual. Being named a lead trainer was viewed as a "promotion" as well as a high honor for longtime outstanding performers.

Think about how you can use this kind of "career-pathing" as a form of recognition/acknowledgment. Knowing the volunteer's motivation for taking the position in the first place will help to guide you. Identify those that would appreciate being acknowledged with new responsibilities or a promotion, and then let the volunteers make the decision about whether or not to accept based on how important what's been offered is to them. Don't make the mistake of thinking, "I couldn't ask her to do one more thing, she's doing so much already." That could keep you from recognizing someone in a very meaningful way.

REAL-LIFE EXAMPLE: RECOGNITION MUST BE MEANINGFUL TO THE VOLUNTEER

I worked with one volunteer for a long time who was well known for his service to the community. He had many awards from several local organizations, and he was originally from New Orleans. He would call my voicemail periodically and tell a gruesome story about eating crawdads—it's the custom to pull off their heads, suck out the juice . . . you get the picture . . .

I happened to vacation in New Orleans one time and spotted a large postcard with this ritual depicted as a cartoon. After buying the card, I addressed it to the parts of his business address I could remember (I guessed at the street number and zip code) and then mailed it: "Dear Bob, Having a great time in your hometown. Wish you were here."

On that survey I mentioned, when asked what was the best way he had ever been recognized for volunteer service, this high-profile community volunteer said: "Carla Lehn once sent me a postcard from my hometown." With all the plaques and crystal trophies he had been given by numerous organizations over the years, he found my postcard the best recognition he had ever received. Why? Because it was personally meaningful to him.

REAL-LIFE EXAMPLE: SPECIAL OPPORTUNITIES AS RECOGNITION

The public relations specialist volunteer mentioned previously felt recognized in three separate situations: First, when he got the opportunity to present his campaign plan to the state librarian, then when the state librarian referred him to a high-level individual in another state department to represent us on a collaboration opportunity, and third, when he came to a public event at the library and the state librarian crossed the crowded room to say hello and meet his wife.

Our volunteer assistant volunteer coordinator felt recognized when she had the opportunity to learn about how to use the volunteer management system, Volgistics, and also when we invited her for a behind the scenes tour of the library's special collections.

When a nearby library asked their book mender volunteers how they wanted to be thanked, they said they would love to learn bookbinding, so the library director made arrangements for them to do that.

REAL-LIFE EXAMPLE: SPECIAL EFFORTS TO ACKNOWLEDGE VOLUNTEERS

A friend in Hawaii made some very special efforts to thank her volunteers. During National Volunteer Week, she wrote a special letter for each—to their child, their significant other, or their employer (with permission), recognizing them for their volunteer efforts and outlining the impact they were making in their community.

The child's letter began something like this: "Dear Megan, Thank you for sharing your mother with us. When she has to miss dinner with you once in a while, she is helping newcomers to our country and our community learn to speak English. When these new neighbors learn English, they can talk to their child's teacher or even get a better job to support their family . . ."

You get the idea. Although getting a letter like this means something to the child, it means even more to the parent. Recognizing a volunteer's accomplishments with their employer (with the volunteer's permission, of course) is also a powerful way to say thanks.

Some volunteers want to participate in a recognition event, but some don't, and some have schedules that won't allow it. Some want a plaque or a mug, and some would rather you spend that money on something else.

You're not being asked to totally give up what you're currently doing to acknowledge volunteers, but you are being asked to take a good hard look at what you're doing in order to make sure it's working—for everyone.

Let your recognition plans be guided by what motivates the volunteers. If they came motivated to learn something new, or to share what they know, they will feel rewarded by getting the opportunity to do that. The best way for you to thank volunteers is to be sure that what you're doing is meaningful to them!

SUCCESS FACTOR 8: SUSTAINABILITY STRATEGIES

In the old "volunteer management" days, the goal was volunteer retention—how can we keep them as long as possible? Success of a volunteer program was partly based on "retention rate." Volunteer recognition programs were guided by how many hours or how many years someone had served.

In her 2017 article, "Sustainability and Volunteerism," Meridian Swift suggests we embrace the sustainability concept by upgrading old volunteer retention approaches. Where we once only focused on making volunteers feel welcomed, and provided cards, gifts, and annual luncheons, we should now be finding ways to connect volunteers to a mission and showing them the impact of their work. "What is the difference then, between retention and sustainability? Well, we've been moving away from the strategies that worked with the WWII generation for some time now. Why not update our verbiage to match the creative ideas being implemented out there."[7]

The trend with today's volunteer is that the person doesn't necessarily see this volunteer position with this organization as a long-term assignment. A skilled volunteer in particular may just come on for a specific project or timeline. We won't be giving out as many 20-year pins in the years to come.

All of the success factors discussed so far—matching the volunteer's skills with the right job, providing training and advancement opportunities, etc.—will certainly contribute to a volunteer staying longer.

But what we need to focus on today is not how to keep the same volunteers toiling every Tuesday night until they step into the grave, but instead we need to think strategically about how we sustain the work when volunteers move on—that's sustainability.

Sustainability Strategy 1: Substitute Positions

My Mom was a Meals on Wheels volunteer. She had a specific route she delivered one day each week. When my family and I moved to Hawaii, she didn't want to be tied down to a weekly shift because she wanted to be free to travel, so she called Meals on Wheels to explain why she would need to leave her position. To her surprise, they offered her the opportunity to be a substitute driver. When another volunteer called in sick or was out of town, she would be on a list of people who could be contacted on short notice to drive that route if they were available. She jumped at the chance, because she loved the assignment—she just didn't want to be tied down to it.

Think about what positions you could create substitutes for—computer coaches or homebound delivery volunteers who could fill in when needed. Having a substitute program provides flexible options for potential volunteers, while solving a problem for the library.

Sustainability Strategy 2: Break Assignments into Smaller Pieces

Having more than one person working on pieces of a project makes it easier if you lose one, because you don't lose total ability to maintain work on the project. It may slow down a bit while those remaining adjust or while you recruit a replacement, but the whole assignment doesn't just drop into your lap because a volunteer leaves.

Sustainability Strategy 3: Job Share

Can two people share a job? If you have a need for data entry several times a week, consider training two people—one to come in on Tuesdays and one on Thursdays. You'll probably want them to get to know each other a bit so they connect and have confidence in the person they're working with, who they may not see very often. Also, be sure they have a system for keeping track of who's done what and what needs to be done next.

If one leaves, you're not left empty-handed. The work continues at a slower pace until you can find a replacement, and the remaining volunteer can also be helpful in training the new person.

Sustainability Strategy 4: Team Assignments

Consider giving a group responsibility for a task and have them manage the work. The Monrovia Public Library's volunteer engagement team described in Chapter 3 was constituted to take on some of the activities of the library's part-time volunteer coordinator—one oversees the computer coach volunteers, one oversees the adult literacy volunteer tutors, the third fields requests for volunteers from staff, and as a team they organize recognition activities.

This team meets regularly with the staff member to coordinate activities and share ideas. If one of the members had to leave for some reason, the others would know enough to hold down the fort until a replacement is found, and the full weight of the responsibility is not left on the part-time staff member.

Sustainability Strategy 5: Consultant Positions

Sometimes a short-term position will be created to achieve a specific task—a graphic designer or photographer, for example. Recruit them as volunteer consultants who can provide expertise when the need arises. They're not necessarily active volunteers all year long, but may be willing to be called on for their skills when you have a need and it fits into their schedule.

Sustainability Strategy 6: Seasonal Volunteers

You may be in an area where "snow birds" come to a warm climate for the winter to get away from the snow, or vacationers spend summers in your town. These folks are often interested in feeling more a part of a community they call home part of the year.

Consider creating opportunities for people to be put to work on things you need when they're available. Some will have skills to share, or be there long enough to be trained to do ongoing tasks, but others might be interested in just doing something you need done to feel part of the community. Things you need year-round could be prepared ahead and in bulk by visitors who'd like to be helpful and might get a chance to meet locals. Do you have packets that need assembling? Early learning kits that need to be packed? Consider using those part-time community members to help you stock up.

This strategy of helping you "stock up" could also be successfully implemented with local community groups you might engage to come in for a few hours a couple times a year. Think Girl Scout or Boy Scout troops, church groups, book clubs, etc., for recruitment ideas.

Sustainability Strategy 7: Two-Deep Leadership

Before I came to libraries, I worked for United Way, which is where I first gained experience with volunteer engagement. A valuable lesson was learned in the concept of two-deep leadership—never have a key volunteer position without someone in training for it. Job transfers, personal illness, or sick relatives to be cared for across the country can't be predicted, so it's always a good idea to have a vice chair or assistant position attached to important volunteer assignments. Someone training in the wings to take over in the future is a great way to prepare for that future—whether it arrives next year as planned or next month because of an unavoidable situation.

The Long-Term Sustainability Strategy: Reach Out to Younger Volunteers

Sustaining success with engaging skilled volunteers for the library who become strong library advocates and supporters will require the engagement of the next generations of volunteers.

Use the generational trends information shared in Chapter 2 to tailor your approach to potential gen X and millennial volunteers. The research clearly demonstrates that they are willing and able to volunteer if approached and treated in ways that make sense to them.

CHAPTER SUMMARY

The eight success factors for volunteer engagement described in this chapter, and the two chapters preceding it, will guide you through steps that will help to avoid problems, while securing for your library the precious time and expertise of community members. Engaging their talents and interests, preparing them to be successful, and acknowledging their work in meaningful ways will help them to feel part of the library family, and they will grow into strong library supporters and advocates.

NOTES

1. Jessica Reade, assistant volunteer coordinator at the Roseville Public Library, describes what happened when they added volunteer interviews to their process in an 87-second video here: http://www.youtube.com/watch?v=n1FjBOxu7ss (accessed March 27, 2017).
2. Kosarin, Elisa, "How an Old Interview Approach Increased Our Volunteer Retention by 30%." https://www.wildapricot.com/blogs/newsblog/2017/03/06/volunteer-interview-retention (accessed April 11, 2017).
3. Zwetzig, Katie, "The Volunteer Interview: Making the Offer . . . or Not." http://verifiedvolunteers.com/Resources/OurBlog/2016/July/The-Volunteer-Interview-Making-the-offer-or-not (accessed May 11, 2017).
4. Kosarin, Elisa, "How to Turn Away Volunteers and Still Have an OK Day." http://twentyhats.com/how-to-turn-away-volunteers-and-still-have-an-ok-day (accessed October 19, 2017).
5. Ibid.
6. Dixon, Andrea, and Melanie Hientz, "2013 Volunteer Recognition Study," 2013, Volunteer Canada. https://volunteer.ca/content/2013-volunteer-recognition-study (accessed October 18, 2017).
7. Swift, Meridian, "Sustainability and Volunteerism," 2017. https://volunteerplaintalk.com/2017/08/23/sustainability-and-volunteerism (accessed October 17, 2017).

Volunteer Orientation and Training Outline

Volunteers should receive *both* orientation to the organization and specific skills training for their assignment. Orientation and training can be done one-on-one or in a group, but both must be done. Sufficient, but not overwhelming, written materials should be provided and referred to during these sessions, but written materials should not take the place of orientation and training.

Volunteer Orientation Learning Goals:

During the session, participants will:

- Be made to feel welcome and an important part of the organization.
- Gain an understanding of the mission and goals of the organization—what it's trying to accomplish and for whom.
- Be introduced to the services provided and major activities and events sponsored by the organization.
- Gain an understanding of how the organization is structured and how volunteers fit into the structure.
- Be briefed on the volunteer program's mission statement, as well as any policies and procedures that affect them.
- Have a tour of the facility.

Volunteer Skills Training Learning Goals:

During the session, the trainees will gain an understanding of:

- The purpose of their position and how it fits into the "big picture" of the organization's service delivery
- The specific job responsibilities and how to accomplish them
- What authority they have in their position
- With whom they will be working and how their job fits with others.
- What to do in an emergency.

Volunteer Public Relations Specialist Job Description

CALIFORNIA STATE LIBRARY

Position Overview and Impact: Guide the development of a statewide public relations campaign during a month-long celebration in honor of the 30th anniversary of California Library Literacy Services in September 2014. The objectives of the project are (1) to increase public awareness about adult literacy (most people know and understand low literacy in children, but not in adults); and (2) to assist in recruiting volunteers to be trained as tutors in order to eliminate waiting lists and serve more adults.

Ongoing Library Contact: Carla Lehn

Key Responsibilities:

1. Assist in identifying key message strategies using our logo, events being held around the state, new video pieces of learners and tutors, and our tag line: "*California Library Literacy Services: Build Skills. Change Lives. Get Involved.*"
2. Develop a statewide public relations campaign to get the message out through media outlets and social media, with very little budget, but with support from library literacy staff and volunteers throughout the state.

Qualifications:

- Willingness to gain an understanding of California Library Literacy Services mission and services
- 5+years experience and demonstrated success in designing public relations campaigns, preferably regional or statewide

Training Provided: Orientation to California Library Literacy Services, and regular meetings with the project director and statewide 30th anniversary team to plan activities, monitor progress and provide data, background information, and problem-solving support.

30th Anniversary Toolkit: http://libraryliteracy.org/staff/resources/30_anv/index.html

Benefits to Volunteer: Use your professional skills to assist in raising awareness of a much overlooked societal problem, and attract potential volunteers to the project who can help to change even more people's lives.

Time Commitment: 3–5 hours per week for eight months

Initial Contact Person: Carla Lehn, Library Programs Consultant

Date Revised: 1/30/14

6

How It All Gets Done

The Edward M. Kennedy Serve America Act[1] was signed by President Obama in 2009 and greatly expanded national service programs. About the same time, a 26-member council of key service leaders convened as "Reimagining Service" and defined four principles to guide their work.

Principle 4 states: "In order to get a return, you have to invest. Organizations that make volunteers central to their work and manage them well are able to generate as much as three to six times the community value from volunteers as the cost to manage them. This is a smart way to maximize impact, but it requires upfront and ongoing financial investment in volunteer engagement . . ."[2]

Whether large or small, libraries that are successful at volunteer engagement have found that there is no substitute for hiring a paid part- or full-time coordinator to oversee their efforts. Instead of bringing someone in from the outside, some have reorganized a current staff member's workload to include all or a portion of their time in this role. Regardless of which of these approaches your library takes, it is critically important that a staff person has been assigned to be the leader of volunteer engagement.

The volunteer engagement coordinator is the primary implementer but can't be the only one working on engaging volunteer talent. Successful volunteer engagement requires participation by others, including staff, director, and trustees.

In Chapter 1, the concept of constituting a volunteer engagement team was raised as a good approach. The team consists of the volunteer engagement leader, the library director (or his/her senior management designee), key staff and volunteers, and a union representative if applicable, and it's also desirable to include members of the Friends group and the board. The team serves as the planning group for beginning or growing your efforts. They bring their own ideas, as well as perspectives from across the organization, and can be used as planners, sounding boards, implementers, and communicators to other staff and volunteers.

In the Appendices for this chapter, you'll find a matrix entitled "Roles in Volunteer Engagement." The left-hand column identifies responsibility areas in volunteer engagement, and columns to the right identify responsibilities for the key players in this process: the library director, the trustees, the volunteer engagement coordinator, and the staff. The key players are discussed below.

ROLES FOR THE LIBRARY DIRECTOR

Volunteer engagement cannot be successful without commitment from the top. Staff will be much more likely to see it as important if it's clear that the library director does.

She or he must be involved from the beginning and should speak at staff meetings about why volunteer engagement is important: to enhance or expand services, attract needed skills, and engage new library supporters and advocates. The director must also speak about his or her commitment to its success and demonstrate that through a commitment of resources, including an assigned staff member in charge, an internal team to work on it, and some financial resources.

Volunteer engagement goals should reflect the support provided by the library. If only 10 percent of a staff member's time is committed to it, only modest outcomes can be expected. On the other hand, if a half- or full-time position is created, higher expectations can be established.

The library director establishes the tone when he or she leads by example. Including volunteer engagement goals in the library's strategic plan sends a message about its importance to the organization. Providing a seat at the strategic planning table for the volunteer engagement coordinator ensures development of volunteer roles in support of the library's strategic goals.

Having a volunteer(s) assigned to work with the director, such as a skilled volunteer in public relations or marketing, demonstrates to staff that volunteer engagement is a high priority.

Another clear signal from the director that volunteer engagement is important is to include it in staff performance reviews, while providing staff time and training to make it work.

Review the role matrix in the Appendices to see the many other ways your library's director can support the implementation of successful volunteer engagement.

A terrific example of a library director leading the charge on volunteer engagement comes from former Roseville, California, library director Rachel Delgadillo. You may want to view a short video of Rachel describing how she worked to overcome the children's librarians' resistance to including volunteers in their plans to expand storytime.[3]

You may also wish to read and recommend Betty Stalling's 2014 article, "12 Key Actions of Volunteer Program Champions: CEOs Who Lead the Way,"[4] to leadership—library director, senior management, and board—which describes things leadership can do to ensure success with volunteer engagement.

ROLES FOR THE BOARD

Rarely do boards raise the subject of volunteers, as if the board has no role. But as discussed in Chapter 1, there are important reasons why the board should be interested and involved:

- Volunteers can help to enhance or expand library services.
- Volunteers bring with them their community connections.
- Volunteers can offer their skills where needed.
- Engaged volunteers naturally transform into strong library supporters.

The board should at least be involved in review and approval of any mission statement developed for volunteer engagement. As described in Chapter 1, it's preferable that you include a board member or two in the group that developed it. This will help them understand the library's purpose in engaging volunteers, as well as that the role of volunteers is to *supplement, not supplant* the role of staff.

If your library is part of local government, there may already be a mission statement for volunteer involvement for use by all departments. If so, the library won't need a separate one, but both board and staff must be educated about it, to be sure they're clear on the thinking behind how the library will be operating.

Another advantage of keeping the board in the loop is that they are often the culprit that says, "Get a volunteer to do it!" when a request is made for additional resources. Ensuring that the board understands volunteer engagement principles will help them understand what is required for success and get their support for what you're working to accomplish.

The board can also be helpful with their personal and community contacts for recruitment and assist with volunteer orientation and recognition as well.

ROLES OF THE VOLUNTEER ENGAGEMENT COORDINATOR, DIRECTOR, OR MANAGER

The roles of volunteer engagement director, coordinator, or manager are neatly described in a column of the role matrix in the Appendices for this chapter. In fact, that column can serve as a draft, sample job description for your use. All the success factors outlined in Chapter 5 are orchestrated by this person. The matrix addresses everyone's role in every aspect of volunteer engagement, so while the coordinator assures they are all addressed, he or she is not doing them all alone but is also managing the involvement of many others to achieve success.

For example, while the volunteer engagement coordinator makes sure that good policy and procedures are established, that person may not be the one writing them. The library director might assist by asking someone in human resources to help with that, or a couple of volunteer engagement team members might take on the research to see what's included in other library volunteer policies and procedures. Alternatively, a skilled volunteer with a human resources background could assist with the research and drafting of policies and procedures for the team's review, and then finally for the library director and board to review and approve.

Recruitment efforts are overseen by the engagement coordinator who enlists others' help by sharing positions that are being recruited for and the qualifications or skills required. When kept informed, the library director, board members, and staff can use their own contacts to attract potential volunteers with those attributes.

When adding an online recruitment platform to the list of recruitment methods, the coordinator needs to understand how it works, but may or may not be the only person who posts all the volunteer opportunities and receives all the inquiries. You may structure it so that the staff leader of a program or service seeking volunteers, such as literacy, homework help, or a maker initiative, is trained to use the online system and takes the volunteer inquiries that are generated for their program or service. You might even recruit a volunteer to do some of that on your behalf. (See Chapter 3's Appendices for a sample assistant volunteer coordinator job description.)

Whether your coordinator is full-time or part-time, all the success factors must be tended to:

- Well-designed volunteer job descriptions
- Targeted recruitment
- Careful screening
- Orientation as well as training
- A supportive climate with good staff buy-in
- Positive support and collaboration
- Meaningful recognition
- Focus on sustainability strategies

All these factors must be implemented whether you have 1 volunteer or 100.

If the coordinator is full-time, you'll have a full-time, full-fledged volunteer engagement effort. If the person is hired part-time, or if this responsibility is only one of many roles the assigned person plays in the library, you must expect to have more limited results.

A challenge for all volunteer engagement directors is to not spin up the effort bigger and faster than your time and resources allow you to manage it successfully. Especially if you're implementing skilled volunteer engagement for the first time, it's best to start with one or two pilot projects. Find your staff champions—staff members who "get it" and are willing to try it with you. You'll gain experience with these first pilot efforts, and once there are success stories that can be shared, you'll find that other staff will be interested in how they can get some help on a project they care about.

CONSIDERATIONS FOR VOLUNTEER ENGAGEMENT LEADERS

Placement of Volunteer Engagement in the Library's Structure

To make sure that everyone understands that volunteer engagement is not the job of just one person, it's best not to call it a volunteer *program*. That makes it sound separate, when it's really an organization-wide service. Calling it volunteer services or volunteer engagement lends itself to an understanding that those efforts are being undertaken on behalf of *all* programs and departments, just like the human resources, finance, and development offices are services for the whole organization. One way to think of it is that the development office raises financial resources on behalf of the entire library, and the volunteer services or volunteer engagement office raises volunteer resources on behalf of the entire library.

Because the volunteer engagement coordinator needs to learn about and interact with all departments and branch libraries, he or she should report to someone as high up in the organization as possible who understands and is committed to the library being successful with volunteer engagement—preferably the library director, human resources director, or other appropriate member of the management team. Ideally, the volunteer engagement director will serve as part of organizational strategic planning and at least periodically should participate in management team meetings so the person can be prepared to assist in designing volunteer opportunities to advance library goals. Therefore, he or she needs to be as close to the library director as possible in the chain of command.

Clarify the Term "Part-Time"

If you were hired into the role of part-time volunteer engagement coordinator, your hours and role in the organizational structure are probably well defined. However, if you were a current staff member asked to take on the volunteer engagement responsibilities as a new aspect of your job, be sure to get a definition of what "part-time" means. Will you be 50 percent in your old role and the other 50 percent of your time on volunteer engagement? Or 75 percent/25 percent? If the terms aren't specifically defined, problems can arise between expectations on both sides.

Whatever the proposed time percentage breakdown, be sure that expectations are realistic. There should be a clear definition of how your original job responsibilities have been cut back to accommodate the percentage of your time that will now be spent on engaging volunteers. If that's not provided, you might want to draft a new job description for yourself that shows the impact of the additional role, and check in with your supervisor to see that you've made the right assumptions.

You may anticipate that your new responsibilities will include a need to work some evenings and weekends for volunteer recruitment or training, or that you might be out of the library occasionally for outreach or developing partnerships. If that's the case, you'll need to get clarification of how that will affect the other piece of your job in terms of scheduling and coverage.

Who Is/Are Your Supervisor(s)?

Divided job responsibilities might also mean you report to more than one person—one for each part of your job. For example, in the original part of your job, you may report to the children's librarian, and for the volunteer engagement part, you may report directly to the library director. If that's the case, it's important to establish how this will work from the very beginning and not wait for a problem to occur before it's discussed.

Will you receive two separate performance evaluations? Or will they come together to provide just one? Establishing the process and criteria for evaluating your performance in two very different aspects of your job will be helpful to all involved.

Another good thing to establish up front is a schedule of update meetings—perhaps once a month or once a quarter—where you can touch base with your supervisor(s) on how things are going and ask for their ideas, support, or feedback on your plans. This also keeps volunteer engagement efforts front of mind for library management.

What Should Your Title Be?

The title should be clear about your volunteer engagement responsibilities. If you were hired for that purpose alone, that shouldn't be a problem, but if volunteer engagement is only one part of your job, your title should reflect that—for example, director of volunteer engagement and outreach, or reference librarian and volunteer services coordinator.

"If you're going to designate an existing staff member to be in charge . . . consider adapting that person's job title to include indication of responsibility for volunteers, as well. First, this clarifies things for the public. . . . Second, the title change tells the rest of the staff that there has indeed been a change in that employee's function."[5]

Helping Staff to Understand Your Role

Shortly after you're assigned to your new role, it should be announced at a staff meeting. Set the stage by having the library director talk about why this change is being made—that skills and talents of community members can be engaged to benefit library users and the community, and that these volunteers, if engaged well, will become strong library supporters and advocates. Or, perhaps a new library service has been added based on strategic planning. Whatever the reasoning, communicating this to staff helps build support and prevent misunderstandings and conflict.

Be sure the announcement includes how this will change the volunteer engagement coordinator's role in your previous position (if that's the situation) and what role other staff will be asked to play in making the volunteer engagement efforts successful. If other staff may be asked to serve on the volunteer engagement team, let them know that their workload will be adjusted to accommodate that.

If all staff will be required to work with volunteers, that should be disclosed, along with the fact that they will be given time for training for success, they will have the opportunity to suggest potential volunteer assignments for their department, and they will work with the volunteer engagement director to create volunteer job descriptions and training plans for implementation.

What Resources Are Available for Volunteer Engagement?

Chapter 1 identified common myths about volunteers, and one big myth is that volunteers are free. Engaging volunteers can be highly cost effective, but there are costs associated with it—it's not free.

Besides the cost of staff time, other resources must be allocated to a variety of other necessities. Required expenses include telephone and photocopying, office supplies, travel expenses, some funds for volunteer recognition, and for your professional development, as well as potential insurance expenses. (Insurance information is covered in Chapter 7, "Administrative and Legal Issues.")

Beyond that, depending on your situation, you may also need funds for volunteer background checks, for a volunteer management system to keep track of volunteers and their service hours, and to generate reports (more on these in Chapter 7 as well), and in some cases, funds for membership in your local volunteer coordinator professional network or national professional association. (See the Resources Appendix under both local and national organizations.) Additional expenses might include reimbursement of volunteers for mileage or parking, for example, if they will be traveling on the library's behalf.

If resources aren't discussed in the initial meetings about the position, be sure to have a realistic budget drafted by the coordinator for current needs and goals; and share it with the coordinator's supervisor(s) soon after taking over the volunteer engagement role.

But money isn't the only resource you'll need to be effective. Staff time will definitely be required. In addition to providing time for staff to work with volunteers assigned to them, members of the volunteer engagement team must be provided with the time to attend those meetings and to follow up on any research or assignments they take on as part of that. Staff working directly with volunteers will need to be given time for training in volunteer engagement, delegation, and supervision. And if there are a number of staff working with volunteers in various departments and/or branches, make time available for them to meet together with the coordinator and their peers periodically. Assuming that those questions are answered in the affirmative, their supervisors should be made aware of those commitments.

Volunteer Engagement Services Structure

Early on in the process, consider how the library will structure its volunteer engagement efforts. The volunteer engagement manager will be at the center of the structure, of course; but if multiple departments and/or multiple branch locations work with volunteers, decide if the volunteer engagement coordinator will manage all volunteer job design and recruitment for everyone, or if that person will coordinate with a volunteer engagement liaison in each department or branch to accomplish those tasks.

Whether in a small library or a large system, it can be most beneficial to take the latter approach. Identifying someone with interest in each branch or department extends the amount of staff time assigned to volunteer engagement, which helps the program grow. That group of liaisons can also naturally create the volunteer engagement team, for planning, training, and ongoing communication with the rest of the organization.

Having others committed to volunteer involvement throughout the system helps with identifying new possible roles for volunteers, and can bring forward any staff issues, problems, or concerns, to keep their managers informed. In essence, they serve as both implementers and internal ambassadors for volunteer engagement.

It's a good idea to create job descriptions for these liaisons to ensure all concerned are clear on roles and responsibilities. For example, are the liaisons free to design volunteer jobs and do their own recruitment for those? Or do they work with the volunteer engagement coordinator to create job descriptions and then serve on the interview panel once a pool of candidates has been recruited? Is the posting of volunteer opportunities on

VolunteerMatch.org or other online platform handled centrally? Or once their volunteer job description has been reviewed and approved, can a branch liaison post it on the online platform and even directly receive the responses from potential volunteers? (Note: A sample branch volunteer coordinator of volunteer engagement from the San Jose Public Library is available in the Get Involved Clearinghouse.)[6]

Ultimately, the right structure is the one that works for your library, based on goals for volunteer engagement, policies, and procedures, and what staffing and other resources have been allocated to it. More on this can be found in a case study of the King County (Washington) Library System's model for integrating a volunteer program, which can be found in Leslie E. and Glen E. Holt's book *Success with Library Volunteers*.[7]

Regardless of how you structure your volunteer services, it's important to "demonstrate the philosophy that volunteers are not 'yours,' but are an integral part of the entire organization, affecting everyone."[8]

Do You Have Any Responsibility for Friends or Foundation?

It's important to know what relationship your volunteer engagement efforts will have to the work of the Friends of the Library and with the Library Foundation, if there is one. Often, the Friends and the Foundation manage their own efforts, and the library director assumes the role of liaison to them. In other cases, the volunteer engagement coordinator is asked to be the liaison to the Friends or Foundation and/or to coordinate that organization's volunteer engagement as well.

Whatever the situation, it's important to clarify if you have any role with these library support organizations, and if so, ask some questions about your work together. For example, will you be asked to help with recruitment of volunteers for their efforts? Or will you only be responsible for volunteers working in library opportunities? And if you're only responsible for the library volunteers, will you and the Friends and Foundation be referring potential volunteers to each other?

Once you understand what the library director has in mind, it is helpful for both the director and the volunteer engagement coordinator to meet with at least the officers of the Friends and/or Foundation to discuss it fully. They may have an interest in working with you, or they may just want to be separate. Either way, once the relationship is established, there will be less chance of any toes being inadvertently stepped on.

AVOIDING BURNOUT OF THE VOLUNTEER ENGAGEMENT COORDINATOR

Whether full-time or part-time, the job of volunteer engagement coordinator has a lot of moving parts, including dealing with many different people—both those paid to work for the library and those who volunteer their time. There will be pressure from staff who are skeptical about engaging volunteers and by managers who want volunteer resources right now so they can start a new service identified in the strategic plan.

The possibility for burnout is high, so here are a few ideas to help to avoid it:

Have a Job Description

If you weren't given a job description for this role, draft one and hold a meeting with your supervisor(s) for review and approval. (Remember to check the sample in the Appendices to this chapter, as well as several samples in the Get Involved Clearinghouse—endnote 9 in this chapter describes how to search the Clearinghouse for them.)[9]

Have a Plan

Take time to identify priorities based on the library's strategic plan, other organizational needs, resources allocated, and your count of the staff "champions" willing and able to get started. If you have a volunteer engagement team, work with them on the plan, and have it approved by the library director and board. Having a plan not only keeps you focused on critical activities, but if a new assignment is added during the year, it provides a baseline for negotiation about what additional resources will be needed or what might need to be postponed in order to accommodate the new priority.

Learn to Delegate Effectively

Remember that this position must be the *manager* of volunteer engagement efforts, not the one who does everything. The best managers surround themselves with competent people to whom they delegate, not by doing everything themselves.

Start by listing all your tasks. Check off each one that could be done by someone else if you had the right person. Then, draft a job description for a volunteer—or several—to assist by taking on those tasks.

REAL-LIFE EXAMPLE: VOLUNTEER PROJECT LEADER

One librarian I worked with was assigned the role of volunteer engagement coordinator half of the time and spent her other half time in children's services. When we made a list of the tasks on her plate, we found something that didn't necessarily have to be done by her—overseeing the volunteers who did the book repair and cleaning.

The librarian had identified several tasks she had been doing that could potentially be done by someone other than herself—reminding volunteers about when the book repair team was meeting; sorting books needing repair; gathering cleaning, and repairing materials; and then on the meeting day, getting the volunteers started, answering questions, and then putting things away afterward.

During the discussion, I asked her to close her eyes and look around the table at her current book repair volunteers to see if there was someone there who might be able to help. The right person for this job jumped out at her from this reverie—a longtime book repair volunteer, who had regularly demonstrated reliability and organizing skills.

We wrote a job description for a "senior book repair technician," requiring experience with the task, who would oversee the team. As you can see from the volunteer job description in the Appendices to this chapter, the senior book repair technician would be involved with the interviews of new potential book repair technicians, assist with their training, schedule monthly book repair sessions around the volunteers' schedules, gather books needing repair and materials required in advance of each session, attend and oversee each session, and see that materials are put away afterward. (The book repair technician job description is also included in the Appendices to show how it differs from the "senior's" role.)

Now, instead of that librarian directly supervising five or six individual volunteers, she can collaborate with the volunteer senior book repair technician, who ensures things run smoothly. She was able to delegate these responsibilities to a carefully selected volunteer (who felt honored by the promotion!), and was able to use the time saved in her day to start a volunteer computer tutor program that was in her plan.

Of course, this model can be replicated. The idea of a data entry volunteer position to enter volunteer hours and an assistant volunteer coordinator to help with VolunteerMatch was mentioned earlier. A volunteer with a human resource background could be helpful with interviewing and reference checks. If you're responsible for a newsletter, a volunteer graphic artist could design it for you, a volunteer photographer could add interest, and a volunteer writer could help to get it produced. The possibilities are endless.

The thought of someone else completing one of our tasks can sometimes feel threatening. After all, "if you want a job done right, you've got to do it yourself . . . ," right? Absolutely not! That kind of thinking will cause you to burn out, experience slow progress, and potentially alienate staff and volunteers who would like to be part of the solution.

Surrounding yourself with competent, carefully selected volunteers, assigning them to a job that is the right fit, and then supporting and collaborating with them allows you to get more things done, while watching them excel.

Seek Out Professional Development Opportunities

One way to reduce your stress is to learn new techniques and strategies to support your work. The Resources Appendix focuses on some of the resources available to you. Many of them offer training and professional development opportunities.

Regional, national, and international conferences and events are tracked by Energize, Inc.[10]

The Get Involved: Powered by Your Library Clearinghouse[11] is a searchable database that stores materials developed by and for libraries working on volunteer engagement. It includes sample volunteer job descriptions and management tools that can be reviewed and downloaded, as well as archived training sessions on a variety of volunteer engagement topics that can be viewed at your convenience.

Join a Volunteer Coordinator Network or Start One Yourself

There may be a local professional association for volunteer engagement professionals who meet periodically to share ideas and problem solve. Often called DOVIA (Directors of Volunteers in Agencies), there is a list that's maintained by state.[12]

If you don't have the luxury of a network nearby, find a volunteer engagement buddy or two in nearby libraries, in other municipal or county departments, or in one or more local nonprofits. Even if you just meet for coffee with one person once in a while, it's important to have someone to commiserate with.

Peer network associations like NAVPLG (National Association of Volunteer Programs in Local Government) and AL!VE (Association of Leaders in Volunteer Engagement) have websites and Facebook pages to investigate, and there are also a number of free online discussion groups you can join including several on LinkedIn.[13]

A WORD ABOUT UTILIZING A VOLUNTEER AS VOLUNTEER ENGAGEMENT COORDINATOR

I'm often asked if volunteers can be recruited to serve as the coordinator of volunteer engagement. As much as I admire and respect the work of volunteers, I don't recommend it, at least not for the coordinator position. You'll quickly become dependent on them if there's no one else assigned to the volunteer engagement workload. If they are called away to assist an aging parent or sick child, or when they get a paid job, there's no one to pick up the pieces. Reread the job description in this chapter's Appendices—there's a lot required!

A volunteer in that position will be hard to replace because he or she has a very particular set of skills. And, expectations have been raised for both volunteers and staff if that person did a good job. If someone doesn't pick up where that volunteer left off, volunteer engagement will lose its credibility quickly. If you can't pick up those pieces along with the rest of your tasks, those who resisted volunteer engagement initially will be able to say, "See—I told you it wouldn't work."

First and foremost, assigning this role to a staff member tells the organization that volunteer engagement is a priority. And if the position is paid, but that staff member leaves the library, there's money in the budget to replace them.

The best option is to put at least a portion of a staff member's time in charge of volunteer engagement and structure some volunteer positions around that coordinator to help with discharging his or her responsibilities. In Chapter 3's endnote 6 you'll find references to two brief videos from the Monrovia Public Library's Volunteer Management Team describing their work and a volunteer job description for assistant volunteer coordinator in the Appendices for Chapter 3.

Use one or more of the sustainability strategies discussed in Chapter 5. Structure volunteer opportunities that can be assigned to one or more volunteers with particular skills and interests. If two volunteers job share responsibility for data entry of monthly volunteer hours, and one of them leaves, there's still one continuing to do the job, and who can also be helpful training a new recruit.

"If you are lucky enough to have someone available and willing to be a staff member at no salary, by all means accept his or her services. But recognize that you are not necessarily building for the future if you do not *budget* for an employee . . . Volunteers able to give the necessary hours to head a volunteer program are few and far between, and if you end up recruiting, say, five volunteers to share the job—are *you* going to supervise and coordinate them?!"[14]

THE ROLES OF STAFF IN VOLUNTEER ENGAGEMENT

The role matrix in the Appendices for this chapter also contains a column for the roles staff can play in all aspects of volunteer engagement. As you read through it, you'll see that there are things every staff member can do, whether or not they serve as part of the volunteer engagement team. Even those who don't work directly with volunteers can be helpful with some tasks. Through their personal and professional networks, they may be able to identify potential volunteers with specific skills or suggest potential partner organizations. They can also bring their own skills to bear on an appropriate project and can definitely have a hand in whether or not volunteers feel welcome.

The matrix also suggests that a key role of staff is to ask for help when needed. Whether it's to ask for help drafting a volunteer job description, or problem solving about a specific situation or person, empower staff with the knowledge that they are not alone in this endeavor. The volunteer engagement coordinator stands ready to help.

Ongoing communication with all staff about volunteer engagement plans and success stories, as well as engaging them when they show interest or bring forward an idea, will go a long way to help them buy in and be supportive.

Keep them informed through general staff, department, branch, and board meetings, and in internal and external library publications and reports. Nothing breeds success like hearing success stories from the library's volunteer engagement efforts, and if those success stories are told by the library director, they have even more impact.

CHAPTER SUMMARY

Success with volunteer engagement requires an organizational commitment to the concept. Whether beginning or expanding the effort, staffing, resources, and placement of the venture must all be considered. But without careful attention to preparing the organization's people and its culture to embrace the idea, toes can be stepped on and feelings hurt that could derail progress.

Remember, everyone plays a role—it's not all just left up to the person with the volunteer engagement job title. Use this chapter and the role matrix in the Appendices as a playbook for implementation, and as a discussion and training tool with management, board, and staff.

"When volunteers are an afterthought, it can be challenging for everyone involved—but when volunteerism is a part of organizational culture, your efforts will return bigger results. Volunteers will be your ambassadors in the community, your capacity builders, and some of your greatest assets."[15]

NOTES

1. https://www.nationalservice.gov/about/legislation/edward-m-kennedy-serve-america-act (accessed May 17, 2017).
2. http://www.reimaginingservice.com/principles.html (accessed May 17, 2017).
3. https://www.youtube.com/watch?v=irJFqtDHQuE (accessed October 18, 2017).
4. Stallings, Betty, and Reimagining Service, "12 Key Actions of Volunteer Program Champions: CEOs Who Lead the Way," 2014. https://www.energizeinc.com

/store/12_key_actions_volunteer_program_champions_free_pdf (accessed, May 21, 2017).

5. Ellis, Susan, *From the Top Down: The Executive Role in Volunteer Program Success,* rev. ed. (Philadelphia: Energize, 1996).

6. http://www.getinvolvedca.org/resource/management-tools/branch-coordinator-volunteer-engagement-san-jose (accessed February 23, 2018).

7. Holt, Leslie E., and Glen E. Holt, *Success with Library Volunteers* (Santa Barbara, CA: Libraries Unlimited, An Imprint of ABC-CLIO, LLC, 2014).

8. Campbell, Katherine Noyes, and Susan J. Ellis, *The (Help!) I-Don't-Have-Enough-Time Guide to Volunteer Management* (Philadelphia: Energize, 1995).

9. Go to www.getinvolvedclearinghouse.org and click on "Management Tools." On the keyword drop-down menu, select "Volunteer Coordinator Job Descriptions." The search will bring up examples of both full- and part-time library volunteer coordinators for your review.

10. https://energizeinc.com/directory/events/bydate (accessed May 22, 2017).

11. www.getinvolvedclearinghouse.org (accessed May 22, 2017).

12. https://energizeinc.com/directory/professional-associations/north-america (accessed May 24, 2017).

13. https://energizeinc.com/directory/onlinec/discussion (accessed May 24, 2017).

14. Ellis, *From the Top Down.*

15. Johnson, Teri, "Building Capacity: Strategic Volunteer Engagement," 2017. http://www.pointsoflight.org/blog/building-capacity-strategic-volunteer-engagement (accessed May 17, 2017).

Matrix: Roles in Volunteer Engagement

Responsibilities	Library Director	Board of Trustees	Volunteer Engagement Coordinator	Staff
Planning for Volunteer Engagement	• Ensure development of a mission statement for volunteer engagement (or implement existing policy). • Communicate to staff the importance of volunteer engagement, and the intent to supplement, not supplant, staff roles. • Participate on the volunteer engagement team or appoint a senior manager. • Ensure sufficient staff, space and budget are designated. • Provide time for staff to be involved in planning and get the training they need. • Involve volunteer engagement coordinator in the Strategic Planning process.	• Actively participate in the planning process when asked. • Embrace the mission or philosophy for volunteer engagement. • Understand that volunteers supplement, but do not supplant staff.	• With the involvement of the library director, key staff, board, Friends, union rep. and volunteers, develop a mission statement for volunteer engagement. (Or implement existing policy) • Based on the mission statement, the library's strategic plan, and resources available, develop volunteer engagement goals and objectives, monitor progress, and make periodic reports to management and staff. • Ensure that sufficient written policies and procedures are in place, and that they are in concert with any city or county jurisdiction policies, including risk management.	• Actively participate in the planning process when asked. • Express your concerns so they can be addressed. • Maintain an open mind. • If selected as a member of the volunteer engagement team, accept research or task force assignments periodically.

Volunteer Job Descriptions	• Insist on having volunteer job descriptions in writing. • Ensure volunteer roles are developed to assist in reaching strategic plan goals.		• Work with staff to identify and develop a variety of meaningful volunteer jobs. • Develop volunteer roles that assist in reaching the library's strategic plan goals.	• Identify meaningful jobs for volunteers, and ask for help to develop good job descriptions.
Recruitment	• Include volunteer opportunities and accomplishments in reports made to the board and funders, as well as in the library's annual report. • In presentations to decision makers and community groups, include volunteer opportunities and success stories. • Utilize your board and community contacts to assist with recruitment of specific individuals or skills. • Invite the volunteer engagement coordinator to accompany you to meetings or events where recruitment might be possible.	• Showcase volunteer opportunities and success stories at board meetings. • Utilize your community contacts to assist with recruitment of specific individuals or skills.	• Use written job descriptions as the basis for recruitment. • Maintain a targeted recruitment program, utilizing several recruitment methods. • Keep the library director, board, staff and volunteers informed of success stories and recruitment needs so they can assist. • Learn to use at least one online recruitment site; post opportunities and use tools effectively. • Train appropriate staff or volunteers in online recruitment best practices. • Maintain relationships with local volunteer center and/ or other such organizations that can assist your efforts.	• Keep eyes open inside the library for potential volunteers. • Use your community contacts to assist with recruitment of specific individuals or skills.

(*continued*)

Matrix: Roles in Volunteer Engagement (*continued*)

Responsibilities	Library Director	Board of Trustees	Volunteer Engagement Coordinator	Staff
Screening	• Make human resources staff available to the volunteer engagement coordinator. • If properly documented, support decisions made to not accept a volunteer, or to reassign or terminate one. • Provide resources for background checks if the library or its local government jurisdiction requires them for volunteers.		• With the involvement of the library director and human resources, design and implement a screening program for volunteers that includes job descriptions, interview guidelines, problem-solving, and background checks when required. • Include key staff on interview teams for volunteers they will be working with.	• When asked, serve on the interview team for volunteers you will be working with.
Orientation and Training	• Be visible at volunteer orientation events, where possible, and always at in-service events about an emergency, or negative publicity about the library. • Make time available for staff to be trained in volunteer engagement.	• When asked, be visible at volunteer orientation events, and at in-service events about a library emergency, or negative publicity about the library.	• Develop and oversee delivery of both orientation to the library, and training for volunteers that will help them be successful in their roles. • Look for ways to engage staff in designing and/or presenting volunteer training to assist with their ownership of volunteer engagement.	• Be willing to help design and/or present volunteer training in your areas of expertise.

	• Provide opportunities for professional development in volunteer engagement for the volunteer engagement coordinator and other key staff.		• Consider ways to engage skilled trainer volunteers in designing and/or presenting orientation and training. • Make time for your own professional development.	
Supportive Climate/Staff Buy-In	• Communicate importance of volunteer engagement. • Make sure department heads understand their role in ensuring volunteer engagement success. • Provide staff time to engage volunteers. Don't just add it to already full workloads. • Provide staff training in delegation, supervision, and volunteer engagement. • Share volunteer engagement success stories with staff, board, local decision-makers and funders. • Consider including volunteer engagement in staff job descriptions, new employee orientations, and performance evaluations. • Set an example by having volunteers directly assigned to you.	• Share volunteer engagement success stories at board meetings.	• Develop and oversee delivery of training and consultation efforts for staff to ensure understanding and acceptance of volunteer engagement, and to develop skills staff need to successfully carry out their critical role. • Share volunteer success stories with director, board and staff. • Set an example by having volunteers directly assigned to you.	• Help volunteers feel welcome, appreciated, and part of the team. • Share volunteer success stories with staff. • Participate in training to enhance your skills in volunteer engagement. • Ask for help with specific volunteer issues or problems. • Ask for additional training as needed.

(*continued*)

Matrix: Roles in Volunteer Engagement (*continued*)

Responsibilities	Library Director	Board of Trustees	Volunteer Engagement Coordinator	Staff
Feedback/ Collaboration and Support			• Encourage staff to keep you informed of volunteer performance. • Be sure that clear, written agreements are made about a skilled volunteer assignment, including tasks, timeline and resources or constraints. • Be sure staff are aware that you are available to assist when problems arise. • Maintain a relationship with Human Resources for guidance & problem-solving.	• Monitor volunteer performance and coach when needed. • Seek help from the volunteer engagement coordinator when problems arise.
Recognition/ Acknowledgment	• Be visible at volunteer recognition events. • Meet with volunteers who require your input to complete their assignment.	• When asked, be visible at volunteer recognition events.	• Be sure volunteers are apprised of the impact made by their efforts on participants and the community.	• Assist with recognition activities when asked. • Encourage volunteers with whom you work to attend or take advantage of volunteer recognition opportunities.

	• Where possible, make special opportunities such as invitations to high level meetings or community events available as a form of recognition for a volunteer working on a related project.		• Develop a plan for recognition that ensures all volunteers are thanked and is based on what's meaningful to the volunteer. Determine that by survey, interviews or focus groups with volunteers. • Look for ways to provide promotional opportunities or a career path for some volunteer positions. • Don't rely solely on events for recognition, but identify additional special opportunities for volunteer recognition.	
Sustainability	• Keep decision makers and funders informed of volunteer engagement success stories, accomplishments, and resource needs. • Ensure adequate ongoing staff and financial support for volunteer engagement, and provide increases to both when warranted.	• Ensure adequate ongoing staff and financial support for volunteer engagement.	• Keep director, board, and staff informed of volunteer engagement success stories, accomplishments, and resource needs.	• Encourage coworkers to participate in volunteer engagement efforts by sharing your experiences and success stories.

Sample Job Description: Volunteer Engagement Coordinator

PUBLIC LIBRARY

Position Overview and Impact: Assists the library in achieving its mission, enhances services to the public, and increases the library's connections with the community by successfully engaging community members as volunteers, many of whom will become some of the library's most effective ambassadors, supporters, and advocates.

Qualifications:

- Good "people skills"
- Good communication skills
- Skills in program planning and organization
- Ability to delegate effectively
- Understanding of volunteer engagement principles

Responsible to: Library Director

Responsibilities:

1. With the involvement of the library director, key staff, board, Friends, union representative, and volunteers, develop a mission statement for volunteer engagement (or implement any existing library, city, or county policy).
2. Based on the mission statement, the library's strategic plan, and resources available, develop volunteer engagement goals and objectives, monitor progress, and make periodic reports to management and staff.
3. Ensure that sufficient written policies and procedures are in place, and that they are in concert with any city or county jurisdiction policies, including risk management.
4. Work with staff to identify and develop a variety of meaningful jobs and written job descriptions for volunteers.
5. Develop volunteer roles that assist in reaching the library's strategic plan goals.
6. Maintain an active targeted recruitment program, utilizing multiple recruitment methods.
7. Keep the library director, board, staff, and volunteers informed of success stories and recruitment needs so they can assist.
8. Learn to use at least one online recruitment site. Post opportunities and use tools effectively. Train appropriate staff or volunteers in online recruitment best practices.

9. Maintain relationships with local volunteer center and/or other organizations that can assist with volunteer recruitment efforts.
10. With the involvement of the library director and human resources, design and implement a screening program for volunteers that includes job descriptions, interview guidelines, problem solving, and background checks when required.
11. Develop and oversee delivery of both orientation to the library and training for volunteers that will help them be successful in their roles.
12. Look for ways to engage staff and/or volunteers in designing and/or presenting volunteer training.
13. Develop and oversee delivery of training and consultation efforts for staff to ensure understanding and acceptance of volunteer engagement, and to develop skills staff need to successfully carry out their critical role.
14. Gather and share volunteer success stories with library director, board, and staff.
15. Set an example by having volunteers directly assigned to tasks supporting the volunteer engagement effort.
16. Ensure effective feedback, collaboration, and support of volunteers by encouraging staff to report on volunteer performance, and assist in creating clear written volunteer agreements with skilled volunteers. Assist with problem solving as needed.
17. Maintain a relationship with human resources for guidance and problem solving.
18. Develop a plan for recognition that ensures *all* volunteers are thanked. At minimum, recognition plans should apprise volunteers of the impact made by their efforts on participants and the community, and should be meaningful to them. Determine that through interviews, survey, or focus groups with volunteers.
19. Look for ways to provide promotional opportunities or a career path for some volunteer positions.
20. Keep library director informed of volunteer engagement accomplishments and resources needs.

Volunteer Job Description: Senior Book Repair Technician (Volunteer Manager, Book Repair Program)

PUBLIC LIBRARY

Position Overview and Impact: Assist with the management of the volunteer program that maintains best-loved books and materials in good repair, so they can continue to be used by library visitors.

Responsibilities: Under the direction of the Director of Volunteer Services:

1. Serve as part of the interview team for new potential Book Repair Technicians to assess appropriateness for the volunteer assignment, and willingness to make the commitment required.
2. Assist in providing orientation to the Library and Book Repair Technician Training.
3. Schedule monthly book repair sessions based on availability of volunteers.
4. Ensure books needing repair and repair materials are available for monthly book repair sessions.
5. Attend and supervise monthly book repair sessions, and put materials away when done.
6. Make monthly reports to Director of Volunteer Services.

Qualifications:

- Must have been a volunteer Book Repair Technician for a minimum of one year
- Willingness to work closely with the Director of Volunteer Services to ensure the success of the Book Repair Technician program

Ongoing Library Contact: Director of Volunteer Services

Training and Support Provided: Periodic meetings with Director of Volunteer Services to plan activities, monitor progress, and provide problem-solving support.

Benefits of Volunteering:

- Provide a much-needed service to library visitors by monitoring the program which ensures that best-loved books are continually available.
- Utilize or gain skills in program management.
- Meet people who share similar interests.

Time Commitment: 8 to 10 hours per month

Length of Commitment: Minimum six-month commitment requested

Grounds for Termination:

- Failure to carry out assigned responsibilities
- Misrepresenting the library or its policies

Initial Contact Person: Susan Good, Director of Volunteer Services, 555-5980

Date Revised: 5/17

Volunteer Job Description: Book Repair Technician

PUBLIC LIBRARY

Position Overview and Impact: Assists in maintaining best-loved books and materials in good repair, so they can be used by library visitors.

Responsibilities:

1. Attend a 3-hour training provided by the library at no charge, on book repair and cleaning.
2. Work with other Book Repair Technicians to set a monthly mending date.
3. Attend monthly mending date, or give your library contact sufficient notice if unable to attend.

Qualifications:

- Good small motor skills and eyesight
- Good attention to detail
- Willingness to work with a small group

Ongoing Library Contact: Senior Book Repair Technician

Training and Support Provided: Orientation to the library as well as a 3-hour training on skills and techniques for repairing, mending and cleaning library books.

Benefits of Volunteering:

- Provide a much-needed service to library visitors by ensuring best-loved books are continually available.
- Gain skills in book mending and repair.
- Meet people who share similar interests.

Time Commitment: Three hours once a month

Length of Commitment: Minimum six-month commitment requested

Grounds for Termination: Failure to carry out assigned responsibilities

Initial Contact Person: Susan Good, Director of Volunteer Services, 555-5980

Date Revised: (5/17)

7

Administrative and Legal Issues

Many organizational issues have been addressed earlier in this book that will support the implementation of volunteer engagement in your library: For example,

- establishing a mission statement for volunteer engagement (Chapter 1);
- constituting a diverse volunteer engagement planning team (Chapter 1);
- structuring volunteer engagement as an organization-wide service, rather than a program (Chapter 6);
- assigning paid staff to oversee volunteer activities and positioning them well in the organization chart (Chapter 6);
- allocating budget for volunteer engagement services (Chapter 6);
- and the importance of aligning volunteer engagement goals and objectives with the library's strategic plan (Chapter 6).

This chapter deals with some of the administrative and legal issues as well as policy decisions that must be addressed for your volunteer engagement program.

LIABILITY AND RISK MANAGEMENT

"People volunteer for many reasons. . . . Whatever motivates someone to volunteer for your organization, it should be a win-win situation for both parties. . . . However, that can quickly change to remorse or anger if the volunteer sustains an injury or harms another. Every nonprofit wants to provide a safe environment" and "should be committed to taking the steps to balance the risks or dangers . . . with the potential rewards. . . . These volunteer risks should be managed effectively to protect everyone involved . . ."[1]

Although this is an important subject that should be discussed at length while establishing a volunteer engagement service, and should be revisited on a regular basis, it's important not to let the possibility of a problem get in the way of positive outcomes that can be achieved by volunteers.

In her article "Common Sense and Volunteer Involvement" Susan Ellis reminds us that: "Overreaction is akin to worst-case scenario planning. That's when an organization is so afraid of any risk, no matter how slight, it simply decides not to engage volunteers at all in an activity. So, because someone might get hurt or do something wrong, a potentially great service needed by clients or the public is stopped before it starts."[2]

That being said, in our litigious society, it is well worth the effort to understand risk—both for volunteers and for the library, *and* to be aware of protections that can be put in place. I'm not a lawyer, but I can share information about some basic protections that are afforded under the law, and steps that can be taken to minimize risk.

Of course, always be sure to utilize your library's legal counsel for guidance on legal matters. That may be the city or county attorney if your library is a part of one of those jurisdictions.

What Is the Law?

The Volunteer Protection Act of 1997 provides some personal liability protection to volunteers, but only if they were acting within the scope of their volunteer assignment when they committed a negligent act.

However, if the volunteer's act or omission was caused by willful or criminal action, recklessness or indifference to the rights or safety of someone who was harmed, or by gross negligence, there is no protection for him or her under this law. Volunteers are also not protected if harm is caused by their operation of any kind of vehicle.

Regrettably, a false impression has been created that volunteers and organizations can't be sued just because the federal law exists. It's important to understand that most volunteers are liable for harm they cause, and no law protects volunteers if they are guilty of gross negligence or recklessness. Also very important to note is that the organization receives no protection from this law.

Every state has its own law regarding volunteer legal liability, and these laws differ in every state. For example, California code protects unpaid officers and directors of nonprofit corporations from liability for negligence only if the organization has secured general liability insurance at a specified level. You can access information about your state laws through a free app maintained by the Nonprofit Risk Management Center, called "VolunteerProtect," which is available on Google Play and from the App Store.[3]

Best Protections

The best protections are those the organization can control—internal policies, written procedures, and insurance. If your library is part of local government, as mentioned before, you may be operating under its policies and procedures for volunteer engagement, and be covered by their insurance. It is critical that you be informed about both. If the local government does not have policies, draft some,[4] and share them with human resources, as well as the risk manager and legal counsel for review and revision. Through this process you can establish a relationship with those offices, which will help when you need to utilize them when questions or issues arise.

If your library is not part of local government, be sure to create policies,[5] and seek direction from human resources, risk management, legal counsel, and insurance carrier.

Internal Policies and Procedures

Good risk management requires that you identify possible risks and then delineate policy and procedures to mitigate them. Utilizing preventative measures can help you control the risks if a volunteer is injured or injures someone else.

Work with the risk manager in your library (or city or county jurisdiction) to create prevention policies and procedures. Then, train volunteers and staff on what's expected.

Also remember the laws only protect volunteers who are acting within the scope of their responsibilities—another good reason to keep written volunteer job descriptions current, and to ensure that carefully screened volunteers receive good training on this topic. "Managing the risk that volunteers will work inappropriately 'outside the box' of your requirements and expectations begins with a detailed description of the responsibilities for the position."[6]

Additional Screening Procedures

For particular types of volunteer roles, extra steps may need to be taken during the screening process. For example, volunteers who will be driving on the library's behalf should be asked for a valid driver's license and up-to-date vehicle registration as part of their screening.

Consideration should also be given to a volunteer position that requires a license or certification during the screening process. One example might be in any volunteer activities that could lead to injury to volunteers, staff, or participants. "For example, a California nonprofit was found liable for the acts of its volunteer scuba diving instructor after a student drowned.

Nonprofit managers knew the volunteer was not a certified scuba instructor, and the court pointed out that activities that are extra hazardous or inherently dangerous may subject the nonprofit to liability."[7] Although scuba diving might not be offered at your library, consider yoga or other types of instructors you may wish to recruit as volunteers.

More on risk management strategies can be found in a brief article by John C. Patterson.[8] Also, a 2016 "Checklist to Minimize the Most Common Volunteer Risks" by Volunteers Insurance Service includes guidelines that can be applied to positions in which volunteers are asked to lift or carry,[9] which might be of particular interest to libraries who have volunteers shelving books, and Friends groups who have volunteers preparing for a book sale.

Training Procedures

Another procedural prevention step is to include risk management topics in your training for specific volunteer positions. For example, if volunteers will be driving as part of their role, be sure to create guidelines for driver conduct and include coverage of those guidelines in your training.[10]

Provide training on established library safety measures to volunteers who will be working in the library so that they can avoid safety risks.

Establishment of "boundaries" is another good example. Often a library's adult literacy volunteers are trained and then reminded regularly about the importance of maintaining boundaries with their adult student(s). Although warm relationships often naturally form between volunteer tutors and their learner(s), the volunteers need to be aware of appropriate expressions of that relationship. For example, many library literacy programs strongly suggest that tutoring sessions should be held only at the library or in another public setting such as a coffee shop, rather than in the student's home. Not lending money to students is another precaution they are asked to take.

Thinking through appropriate boundaries in certain volunteer positions will go a long way toward keeping volunteers and patrons safe, while not disrupting the personal "bonding" aspect of the position that is often very important to the service.

Insurance

Insurance coverage is the third protection mechanism. Check with your risk manager or insurance provider to be sure that sufficient insurance is carried, and that it includes specific coverage for volunteers.

"Consider risk management to be an entire system of ways of dealing with risks, of which insurance makes up only one component . . . insurance only helps once a loss has happened. It's not designed to prevent losses . . ."[11]

A WORD ABOUT BACKGROUND CHECKS

Libraries should seriously consider their responsibility to take steps to ensure that their service recipients are protected from harm. Staff and volunteers who work with vulnerable populations should be carefully screened, and sometimes that will include checking criminal history records.

When to Do a Background Check

Unless a background check for every volunteer is mandated by your local government jurisdiction, or by your library itself, consider identifying which volunteer positions, if any, should require a background check.

"Always base the screening process on the risks posed by the position. Your analysis of the position description should lead to the selection of appropriate screening tools. For example, a volunteer position requiring unsupervised, one-to-one contact with a vulnerable client is a high-risk position. A volunteer position whose duties include answering phones in a busy office may be considered a low-risk position depending on the organization."[12]

Examples of positions to consider requiring a background check for include those working with children and homebound patrons.

Who Will Do Your Background Checks?

Once positions that require a background check have been identified, start your search for a background check provider by talking to local law enforcement. They will sometimes provide this service free or for a nominal fee to other departments in their local government and/or for local organizations. More options for obtaining such information are detailed in an article by the Privacy Rights Clearinghouse.[13]

Some organizations—especially those with large numbers of volunteers—have begun to contract with professional background screening companies. Often, companies that perform employee screening have programs available specifically for running background checks on potential volunteers and may offer bulk rates.

There are a number of companies that provide this service and some that provide it exclusively for volunteers. Do some research and talk with your network of volunteer engagement contacts about who they work with to find the best match for your situation.

Treat Applicants Fairly

Applicants should be treated fairly and their privacy must be respected, so be sure you have procedures in place to accomplish those things. Also make sure that any confirmed offenses are relevant to the volunteer position for which they've applied. For example, a felony conviction for embezzlement should help to screen out a volunteer whose position would require them to handle money or teach financial management, but it might not be relevant to a volunteer position repairing or shelving books.

In its article "Checking Criminal Histories: Considerations before You Begin," the Nonprofit Risk Management Center states: "A criminal history record check is part of a screening process—not a selection criterion . . . clear guidelines stating which offenses are relevant; what offenses will disqualify an applicant; what other factors will be considered; and how the rights of the applicant will be preserved."[14]

Criminal history databases are not perfect and may falsely identify that someone has a criminal record. If applicants challenge the accuracy of any information you receive, you must give them the opportunity to contact the source of the information to resolve any disputes. It's best that they work on the resolution rather than you.

Will Potential Volunteers Be Turned Off by All This?

There has been a perception that doing background checks on volunteers is invasive and will keep good potential volunteers from applying for a position. Over time, however, those concerns seem to have moderated as our world has changed.

A survey conducted between December 2016 and February 2017 asked volunteers how they felt about having their identities verified. Ninety-one percent expressed neutral or positive feelings about identity verification, and 8 out of 10 said they were more likely to volunteer for an organization that requires identity verification.[15]

Who Pays for the Background Check?

It's certainly nice when the organization pays the cost of a required background check, but that's not required. Some libraries or the local government they are part of set funds aside in their budget for it, but it's also not unheard of for an organization to ask the volunteer to cover the cost.

As a volunteer, I am asked to cover the cost of a background check every five years for an organization I volunteer for. They use one of the commercial providers. This year (2017) the cost to me was $8, and it was easy to complete the process and pay online without leaving my desk.

If you will be asking volunteers to pay for their background check, be sure they know in advance and are apprised of the reason for doing it, and the cost, as well as the process for completing it.

DATA MANAGEMENT

Spend some time thinking about what records need to be kept about volunteers and their engagement with the library. You'll certainly want a baseline of information on each volunteer—at least contact information—probably e-mail, phone, and address—and volunteer position, start date, and emergency contact information. You may also need to keep copies of documents such as their application, and other forms that you require their signature on, such as a volunteer agreement or confidentiality agreement, as well as a criminal history background check if required for the position.

There will most likely be a need to create reports on volunteer activities—at minimum, the number of volunteers and number of volunteer hours contributed. You might also want to be able to detail the number of volunteers and hours by assignment, department, or branch.

Minimal information on a small number of volunteers can be maintained on a spreadsheet or even on paper. If maintained in one of these ways, however, be sure that personal information is handled carefully. Talk to human resources about the best way to store it.

As your volunteer engagement activities grow, however, you might want to investigate maintaining the information electronically by using a volunteer management system (VMS). There are a variety of products available, so you'll want to think through what features and functions are important before deciding which to invest in. Jayne Cravens of Coyote Communications maintains a useful list.[16]

Features and functions available in VMS products include:

- **Volunteer profile.** Contact and other information about each volunteer.
- **Tracking capability.** What each volunteer does, when and how much.
- **Scheduling.** Do you need the capacity to schedule volunteers? Or to have them schedule themselves?
- **Search features.** Ability to search by skills, interests, or qualifications.
- **E-mail function.** Some allow you to contact volunteers from within the system.
- **Communication/mailing.** Create e-mail merges and mailing labels.
- **Generate reports.** What kind of reports will you require?
- **Online capability.** Some VMS products include the capability of having new volunteers complete their application and/or for existing volunteers to select their schedules, report hours, and/or change their information online.

Think through what your data and reporting needs will be, talk to other volunteer engagement contacts about what system they use, and then do some research. Three good sources of VMS research are:

- Idealware's[17] Consumer's Guide to Software for Volunteer Management.
- VolunteerPro archived webinar: Online Volunteer Management Software Expo.[18]
- Get Involved Clearinghouse.[19]

MEASURING SUCCESS

So, is all this extra activity surrounding volunteer engagement worth it? This is an important question to ask yourself, because you'll be asked by others—by management, by other staff, by board members, and by funders.

Even if you're not being asked for the information, report it anyway! In her article "Inform, and WOW, Everyone about Volunteers," Susan Ellis reminds us that, "What we do not measure, we do not value. . . . If you have been asked to report only limited information (e.g., head count, hours served) keep giving that data but add more important stuff that will make your report POP."[20] (Read on for examples of the "important stuff" you can add.)

The ability to demonstrate how much volunteers accomplish on behalf of the library is invaluable—you can share it with management to help justify additional resources; share it with staff to gain their enthusiasm and buy-in; and share it with volunteers to make sure they're aware of their significant contributions. (Remember from Chapter 5 the 2013 study by Volunteer Canada found that the top way volunteers want to be recognized—80 percent—is to hear about how their work has made a difference.)[21]

Select the measurements you will use by determining which are both meaningful to you and that you can realistically gather data on. Then start sharing your results through written reports to library management, oral reports at board meetings, in staff meetings, in newsletters, on social media, in presentations at service clubs, and in the library's annual report.

Measuring Outputs (Things You Can Count)

The most basic data to collect is the number of volunteers who served and the total number of hours they spend volunteering for the library. You'll want to track this information over time to show how volunteer engagement is growing. And if it's not growing, you can do some analysis about why it's not: Were resources cut? Was there staff turnover? Do you need to review your recruitment methods?

A next simple step that many volunteer engagement coordinators take is to demonstrate the dollar value of the volunteers' time. The nonprofit Independent Sector annually calculates the estimated value of a volunteer hour to assist organizations in quantifying the value volunteers provide.[22] They present both the national average and state values you can use to multiply by the number of total volunteer hours to get a monetary value. Just be sure for consistency that whichever value you pick—national or state average—gets used each year.

Consider what other outputs of your volunteer efforts you can count and report on that will help to put those numbers in context. For example:

How many third graders were read to by a volunteer? How many low-literate adults were helped by a volunteer tutor? How many tours of your facility did docents lead, and for how many participants? How many individuals were helped by a volunteer computer coach? How many library Friends participated in the book sale, and how much money was raised?

Reporting only the numbers of things you can count won't be as meaningful to the people you share the information with if you don't add some examples of what volunteers do to support the library's mission.

Anecdotal Information

Including succinct and compelling anecdotes in your reporting will help bring the data alive. Have some brief stories ready to personalize your results, whether you're writing or speaking about them. Here are a couple of examples:

When the company Luis worked for went belly-up, he spent many hours on the computers at the library looking for work. He was chagrined to see that some Latinos toiled over how to use computers.

Luis, who is bilingual, started helping to translate for those he saw struggling. His background is in computers, so once he was successful finding a job, he started as a volunteer, teaching a computer class in Spanish at the library.

The library's Homework Club Program has a volunteer tutor coordinator who is responsible for recruiting, scheduling, and engaging high school volunteer tutors who work with elementary school students who drop in. A satisfied parent shared this comment: "I was having the most difficult time getting my daughter to do homework. Since we discovered the Homework Club, homework for my daughter has become more enjoyable. I cannot express her enthusiasm about this club. She actually reminds me that Monday is time to go to the library. As a matter of fact, she has told everyone she can that they should go to the Homework Club at the library. I could not be happier about this fabulous opportunity my child has been provided with. The volunteer tutors have done a tremendous job. My daughter has gone from practically hating homework to actually looking forward to doing it."

Volunteers with Friends of the Library raised $35,000 at their book sale this year. The funds were provided to the library to start a Reach Out and Read program in partnership with a local health *clinic. Reach Out and Read recognizes pediatric checkups as an opportunity for doctors and nurses to discuss the importance of parents reading to their children. In addition, volunteers will read aloud in the pediatric waiting room, and free children's books will be given to families at each well-baby visit.*

Highlighting your numbers with brief stories like these will help others understand what you already know—that volunteers provide important services to the community on the library's behalf.

Return on Investment

Are you ever asked to justify the staff time and other resources allotted to your volunteer engagement program? Or do you have the need to justify an increase in those resources? If so, you can take the value of volunteer time to the next level by calculating the return on investment (ROI) of your volunteer engagement activities.

In 2010, the National Council on Aging produced a report[23] demonstrating that the return on investment in attracting, engaging, and managing leadership-level volunteers is ". . . strikingly impressive." Organizations around the country who participated in the study "achieved an average return-on-investment of nearly 800 percent." In other words, for every dollar invested, almost $8 in value was returned.

If you'd like to be able to measure and share that kind of information, then ROI is something to explore. It doesn't have to be terribly difficult or complex. Tobi Johnson of VolunteerPro describes the basic formula: ROI = (volunteer value − program cost) / program cost.[24]

Tobi suggests that you use the steps to follow for your calculation (or sign up for her e-mailed weekly tips, and she'll send you her return on investment calculator).[25]

Here's a brief summary of the steps to take:

1. **Calculate program costs.** List and total all costs for your volunteer engagement service, including but not limited to staff time assigned (remember, if it's 25 percent of a full-time person, use just 25 percent of the salary); staff benefits (again, based on percentage time of staff assigned); office supplies; travel costs; training; recognition expenses; etc.
2. **Calculate volunteer value.** Take the volunteer hours (total) for last year and multiply by the value volunteer time figure, mentioned earlier.[26] Select either the national figure or the figure for your state, but whichever you choose, be sure to use that choice each year you do the calculation.
3. **Calculate ROI.** Subtract program costs from volunteer value, then divide that by the program costs. ROI = (volunteer value − program cost) / program cost.

Measuring Outcomes (What Difference It Made)

Reporting only the number of volunteers and volunteer hours, even including volunteer hours expressed as a dollar value, may still leave your reader or listener wondering what difference that makes.

"Typically, volunteer programs share results that consist solely of numbers. These results would be much more telling if someone had asked this question: 'So what?' For example, if 10 volunteers put in 500 hours this quarter, and that's an increase of 5 percent over last year—so what? Why is this significant? What change did they accomplish?" (Kanter, 2015).[27]

In her article "Documenting the Difference: Demonstrating the Value of Libraries through Outcome Measurement,"[28] Peggy D. Rudd, former director and librarian, Texas State Library and Archives Commission, defines outcomes this way:

> Outcomes—Benefits or changes for individuals or populations during or after participating in program activities, including new knowledge, increased skills, changed attitudes or values, modified behavior, improved condition or altered status (e.g., number of children who learned a finger play during story time, . . . number of students whose grades improved after homework clinics, . . . number of people reporting being better able to access and use networked information after attending information literacy classes).

When you report the number of children who participated in story time, you're reporting "outputs"—just the number of children attending. By adding information about what those children were able to do differently after story time—they learned to do a finger play—you're reporting "outcomes."

The ability to share outcomes—measurements of a change made in knowledge, skills, attitudes, or behavior—answers the "So what?" question by describing the *difference that was made*.

Here are two examples from the "Measuring Outputs" section above of how you might extrapolate "outputs" to "outcomes" by gathering some additional information:

- **How were individuals helped by the volunteer computer coaches?** Instead of just reporting "how many," gathering information about what the individuals who were served by a volunteer actually learned could lead to an outcomes measurement like this: "76 seniors worked with a volunteer computer coach this year. Afterwards, 60 of the seniors were able to send an e-mail, 58 were able to search the Internet, and 42 joined Facebook to keep in touch with family and friends."

  Being able to report this way, of course, would require establishing a data-gathering mechanism that tells you what the participants learned or were able to do differently as a result of the service received.
- **How were low-literate adults helped by a volunteer tutor?** Again, instead of only reporting "how many," meaningful outcomes data here might be a pretest

and posttest of each adult learner to determine reading grade level before and after service, or asking adult learners to establish goals for their reading improvement, and then measure their meeting of those goals, such as "Fill out an application," "Read medicine labels," or "Get a driver's license." (*Note:* California Library Literacy Services has developed an outcome measures process for adult learners called Roles and Goals,[29] which was recognized by the Library of Congress as a 2014 Literacy Awards Best Practice.)[30]

The ability to report on the outcomes of services provided is dependent on the organization's capacity to gather meaningful data that actually measures changes in knowledge, skills, attitudes, or behavior of the people served. If this kind of data gathering is beyond your current capacity, work toward identifying one or two outcomes that you could actually measure for the future, and schedule that as a goal in your volunteer engagement operational plan.

Adding even one outcome into your reporting will have a significant impact on perceptions of the value of your volunteer engagement service. It will also have an impact on reporting results for the service itself. Engage willing program staff in helping to identify data-gathering strategies that will be useful to their reporting as well as yours.

Measuring Progress on Library Strategic Plan Goals

Hopefully you've included volunteer engagement as a tool toward meeting goals in the library's strategic plan, as recommended in Chapter 6. If a goal for the library is that every kindergartener has a library card before reaching first grade, what role could volunteers play in achieving that? If a goal for the library is to reach out to community members who need to improve their ability to speak and read English, what role can volunteers play in carrying that out?

Be sure to report on progress made on those goals. Even if their progress is already included in the library's strategic plan update or annual report as program results, it will serve you well to include that information in reports you make about the roles volunteers play.

Measuring Progress toward Volunteer Engagement Goals

Finally, you want to be able to measure and report on progress toward your volunteer engagement goals.

Volunteer engagement services should have goals and objectives for its own operations as well. Perhaps your library's volunteer engagement service's plan for this year includes goals such as these:

- establish a meaningful written job description for every volunteer position;
- begin implementing volunteer interviewing practices;

- establish three new skilled volunteer positions;
- hold a volunteer recognition event during National Volunteer Week; or
- reach out to two library departments who currently don't utilize volunteers to encourage their participation.

Include in your reporting the progress made toward these goals as well. Staff, management, board members, and volunteers will gain confidence in and respect for volunteer services through this demonstration of professionalism through both program planning and implementation of best practices.

In reviewing your data, you may find that all the results aren't what were hoped. If you were not successful in getting two new library departments to onboard with volunteer engagement, make an assessment of why not. What were their objections to participation? What steps need to be taken to address their objections? What or who could help you convince them to try a pilot project? Maybe you held a volunteer recognition event that those who participated really loved, but only 60 percent of the library's volunteers attended. What steps need to be taken to ensure that all volunteers feel recognized for their service?

Answering questions that arise in your data review will shape goals and objectives for the future. Include those insights in your reporting as well, again to demonstrate professionalism and commitment to improvement. Remember, it's only a failure if you don't try to address the issues that arise.

The Future of Volunteer Impact Measurement

The 2016 book, *Measuring the Impact of Volunteers: A Balanced and Strategic Approach*,[31] has taken the next step in addressing the limitations of traditional measurement tools for volunteer engagement by looking at how it is related to the entire organization.

The authors recognized that employee evaluations are based on how well the staff member adheres to the organizational mission and goals, and determined that the work of volunteers should be aligned as well. By identifying ways in which volunteer engagement supports or could support the mission, and identifying gaps in programming to achieve them, volunteer positions can be designed that satisfy those needs.

By applying an assessment tool well recognized by business and nonprofits called the "balanced scorecard," the authors demonstrate how to capture success indicators for tracking and monitoring of improvements. They created a Volunteer Resources Balanced Scorecard that offers a means of measuring the outcomes and impact of volunteer engagement. The book provides examples and worksheets for taking this next dramatic step toward measuring volunteer impact.

CHAPTER SUMMARY

Considering legal and data management issues helps you protect volunteers, their personal information, and the library itself. Rely on your library's risk management, human resources, legal, and insurance professionals for guidance in this area. Just be careful to not let decision makers rely on the use of risk avoidance as an excuse for not engaging volunteers. Focus on learning how to assess, prevent, avoid, and manage risk to ensure that an important service is available to your community through the engagement of volunteers.

The ability to effectively gather, store, and retrieve data makes reporting on volunteer engagement activities possible and allows volunteer engagement impact and success stories to be shared with management and funders who require reporting, staff who will be energized by it, volunteers who will feel recognized by it, and the community at large who will be impressed by it. So, don't hesitate to shout your successes from the rooftops!

Stretch to go beyond just counting outputs (numbers of things) by adding anecdotal information, return on investment calculations, and hopefully outcome measures (actual changes made). All this data rewards you for your efforts, helps to justify additional resources for volunteer engagement, and also helps to focus future planning.

"When asking 'So what?' come up with answers that can be evaluated, measured, and used to build organizational capacity. These answers will speak to your volunteer program's vision, resources, actions, short-term results, and the sustained outcome and impact your efforts accomplished. And these answers will elevate the conversation by demonstrating powerful, data-informed, and results-orientated volunteer engagement that both inspires and informs ongoing strategy" (Kanter, 2015).[32]

NOTES

1. Nonprofits Insurance Alliance of California and Alliance of Nonprofits for Insurance, "Managing Volunteers: Balancing Risk and Reward." https://www.insurancefornonprofits.org/resources/Booklet-Volunteers.pdf (accessed October 17, 2017).

2. Ellis, Susan, "Common Sense and Volunteer Involvement," 2012. https://www.energizeinc.com/hot-topics/2012/april (accessed October 18, 2017).

3. The Nonprofit Risk Management Center used to maintain a pdf of state volunteer laws on their website, but in 2016 they updated the content in a free app called "VolunteerProtect," which is available on Google Play and from the App Store. The app includes the full text of the Volunteer Protection Act of 1997, as well as specific state laws that provide protection from liability for volunteers. With this app, you can read the federal law and look up the specific laws that apply in your state (app accessed June 3, 2017).

4. You can gather sample policies from surrounding libraries or local nonprofit organizations to help you get started with your own. You can also check the Get

Involved Clearinghouse for a variety of sample policies. Go to www.getinvolved clearinghouse.org, click on "Management Tools," and use the keyword dropdown menu to select the topic you need (accessed June 3, 2017).

5. Ibid.

6. Herman, Melanie L., *No Surprises: Harmonizing Risk and Reward in Volunteer Management*, 5th ed. (Washington D.C.: The Nonprofit Risk Management Center, 2009).

7. Kelley, Siobhan, "Risky Business: There's Liability for the Acts of Your Volunteers," 2014. www.thenonprofittimes.com/news-articles/risky-business-theres-liability -acts-volunteers (accessed October 17, 2017).

8. Patterson, John C., "Does Liability for Negligent Hiring Apply to Volunteers?" https://www.energizeinc.com/art/does-liability-negligent-hiring-apply-volunteers (accessed October 18, 2017).

9. Volunteers Insurance Service, "Checklist to Minimize the Most Common Volunteer Risks," 2016. http://www.cimaworld.com/wp-content/uploads/2016/05/VIS -Connections-Spring-2016.pdf (accessed October 18, 2017).

10. Nonprofit Risk Management Center, "Risk on the Road: Managing Volunteer Driver Exposures." https://www.nonprofitrisk.org/resources/articles/risk-on -the-road-managing-volunteer-driver-exposures (accessed October 20, 2017).

11. Denton, Hal, and Fiona Lally, "Myths of Volunteer Risk Management—Part 2." https://www.nonprofitrisk.org/resources/articles/myths-of-volunteer-risk -management-%C2%8B-part-2 (accessed October 17, 2017).

12. Herman, *No Surprises.*

13. Privacy Rights Clearinghouse, "Volunteer Background Checks: Giving Back without Giving Up on Privacy." https://www.privacyrights.org/consumer-guides/volun teer-background-checks-giving-back-without-giving-privacy#how%20are%20 screened (accessed June 3, 2017).

14. "Nonprofit Risk Management Center, "Checking Criminal Histories: Considerations before You Begin." https://www.nonprofitrisk.org/resources/articles /checking-criminal-histories-considerations-before-you-begin (accessed October 17, 2017).

15. VolunteerMatch/SureID webinar, April 27, 2017. Recording: https://www .youtube.com/watch?v=7ojORZv0bPY (accessed August 7, 2017).

16. A good list of VMS features to consider is maintained by Jayne Cravens of Coyote Communications here: http://www.coyotecommunications.com/tech/vol manage.html (accessed August 7, 2017).

17. Quinn, Laura S., Kyle Henri Andrei, Chris Bernard, and Jay Leslie, "A Consumer's Guide to Software for Volunteer Management: An Overview of Tools for Helping Your Nonprofit or Library Manage Volunteers," 2011. http://www.techsoup .org/support/articles-and-how-tos/consumers-guide-to-software-volunteer-manage ment (accessed August 7, 2017).

18. Johnson, Tobi, VolunteerPro, "Online Volunteer Management Software Expo," October 26, 2016. Presenters from five VMS providers talk about their systems. Archived webinar and comparison matrix available here: http://www.volpro .net/volunteer-management-software-expo (accessed August 7, 2017).

19. Get Involved: Powered by Your Library Clearinghouse of Resources: Go to www.getinvolvedclearinghouse.org, click on "Management Tools," then in the keyword

dropdown menu, select "Volunteer Management Systems" for reviews of specific volunteer tracking systems in use by several California public libraries (accessed August 7, 2017).

20. Ellis, Susan, "Inform, and WOW, Everyone about Volunteers," July 2016. www.energizeinc.com/hot-topics/2016/july (accessed August 4, 2017).

21. Dixon, Andrea, and Melanie Hientz, "2013 Volunteer Recognition Study," Volunteer Canada, 2013. http://volunteer.ca/content/2013-volunteer-recognition-study (accessed June 15, 2017).

22. Independent Sector (Dollar Value Average). https://www.independentsector.org/volunteer_time (accessed August 2, 2017)

23. National Council on Aging, "The Boomer Solution: Skilled Talent to Meet Nonprofit Needs." http://toolkit.encore.org/wp-content/uploads/2016/03/BoomerSolutionSkilledTalent.pdf (accessed August 3, 2017)

24. Johnson, Tobi, VolunteerPro, "Return on Investment (ROI) for Volunteer Programs." http://www.tobijohnson.com/2012/01/08/roi-for-volunteer-programs (accessed August 7, 2017).

25. Johnson, Tobi, "Return on Investment (ROI) Calculator." http://volpro.net/volunteer-roi (accessed August 3, 2017).

26. Independent Sector (Dollar Value Average). https://www.independentsector.org/volunteer_time (accessed August 2, 2017).

27. Rosenthal, Robert J., Ed., *Volunteer Engagement 2.0: Ideas and Insights Changing the World* (Hoboken, NJ: Wiley & Sons, 2015), p. 273.

28. Institute for Museum and Library Services, "Perspectives on Outcome Based Evaluation for Libraries and Museums." https://www.imls.gov/assets/1/AssetManager/PerspectivesOBE.pdf (accessed August 2, 2017).

29. Reinke, Valerie, and Carla Lehn, "Implementing the Roles & Goals Process." http://www.libraryliteracy.org/staff/rg/index.html (accessed August 2, 2017).

30. Library of Congress, "Literacy Awards 2014, Best Practices." http://read.gov/documents/bestpractices2014.pdf (accessed August 2, 2017).

31. Burych, Christine, et al., *Measuring the Impact of Volunteers: A Balanced and Strategic Approach* (Philadelphia: Energize, 2016).

32. Rosenthal, Robert J., Ed., *Volunteer Engagement 2.0: Ideas and Insights Changing the World* (Hoboken, NJ: Wiley & Sons, 2015), p. 274.

8

Volunteer Engagement Strategy Summary

This chapter is a roundup of key success strategies identified throughout the book. Readers can use the strategies as a playbook to help shape their own success regardless of library size, and whether volunteer engagement is being implemented for the first time, or just being enhanced or expanded.

ASK FOR HELP: SEEK INPUT

Establish a volunteer engagement team that includes management, and staff from all parts of the organization, as well as volunteers, including representatives from the board, Friends, and Foundation.

Listen to what they have to say, and together develop a plan to address opportunities and concerns. This will increase ownership of the project by the team, and later gain the trust of other staff and help to overcome their fear of change.

DEMONSTRATE THE POSSIBILITIES

Help people see the possibilities in volunteer engagement. Share volunteer success stories unfolding in other library departments or in other libraries. Seeing what's possible will make them want more.

Not everyone will embrace the expansion of volunteer roles immediately, so start with your "champions"—the people you've identified who see what you're trying to do. Create a "pilot test" with one or more of them, and ask them to share those successes throughout the organization.

GAIN SUPPORT OF MANAGEMENT

Get management on board by sharing what you've learned. Be sure to make the point that this isn't just about getting more of the same traditional volunteer jobs done. It's about enhancing and expanding services, attracting new community members to the library, and watching them naturally become library supporters, ambassadors, and advocates.

ESTABLISH AN UNDERSTANDING OF THE BENEFITS OF VOLUNTEER ENGAGEMENT THROUGHOUT THE ORGANIZATION

Providing training at many levels can make an organization-wide difference. In addition to training the volunteer engagement team, management, and other staff, if you have branch libraries and/or library support groups to engage—board, Friends, and Foundation—you may need to train a variety of individuals and teams in multiple locations.

Use materials provided and resources identified in this book to design training that will get the entire organization excited about implementing a skilled volunteer engagement strategy, and don't forget to share success stories.

DESIGNATE STAFF FOR THE VOLUNTEER ENGAGEMENT EFFORT

There's a correlation between libraries who are successful with this and those that have at least part of a staff person's time to oversee it.

Utilizing a volunteer as the coordinator is not the best approach. Assigning the role to a staff member tells the organization that volunteer engagement is a priority and reduces a gap in services when that staff member leaves, because a salary already exists in the budget.

Paid volunteer engagement leaders, whether full- or part-time, can surround themselves with volunteers who extend their reach by applying their skills to volunteer engagement tasks.

ESTABLISH ROLES FOR VOLUNTEERS

Carefully designed job descriptions help volunteers decide whether or not to take the job and clarify their role vis-à-vis the staff role. Staff will also be comforted by clear delineation of roles and responsibilities, which reduces the number of toes stepped on.

Job description development helps to plan the assignment and identify skills a potential volunteer would need. Engaging staff who will work with this volunteer in developing the job description is also a big step in gaining staff buy-in.

Including the impact—what difference will be made—by the volunteer in the position will also go a long way toward answering a key question that the volunteer of today wants answered.

PLAN, PLAN, PLAN

As mentioned above, a key planning tool is the volunteer job description. Determining roles for volunteers and how they work within the organizational structure is a critical first step in making the right fit.

In addition to planning at that level, however, are three more key planning functions to ensure the success of volunteer engagement: (1) being relevant to the library's strategic plan, (2) being included the library's strategic plan, and (3) creating an operational plan for volunteer engagement.

Be Relevant to the Library's Strategic Plan

Nothing will endear the volunteer engagement service to management, staff, and board more than the ability of volunteers to assist in effectively achieving the library's strategic goals.

Optimally, the volunteer engagement coordinator is a member of the management team, but at the very least, the person should have direct access to the strategic planning process. The opportunity to be involved firsthand as organizational goals develop assists in designing creative volunteer approaches that will enhance the library's chance for strategic goal achievement.

When volunteer engagement is seen as an asset to advancing the library's mission and goals, its position in the organization is enhanced and its sustainability more certain.

Be Included in the Library's Strategic Plan

Make the case for including volunteer engagement goals in the library's strategic plan. There will most likely be broad goals for finance and human resources—such as "Prepare clear, accurate, and timely financial reports which support the board's ability to monitor the library's financial position," or "Utilize hiring, orientation, and training practices which maintain the highest quality staff"—so find a place for volunteer engagement to be highlighted too.

How about this: "Implement a volunteer engagement initiative which seeks community members with skills to share that can effectively supplement, not supplant the work of staff in enhancing and expanding services to the community." Objectives and strategies to achieve that goal can be derived from your volunteer engagement operational plan.

Develop and Monitor an Operational Plan for Volunteer Engagement

In addition to planning for volunteer contributions to organizational strategic goals, the volunteer engagement coordinator (and team) develops at least annual operational plans which identify implementation priorities that ensure development and improvement.

Pinpointing specific steps to take to improve performance will serve as a roadmap for volunteer engagement leadership, will demonstrate to management, staff and volunteers a strong commitment to professional practices, and if a new assignment is added during the year, the plan provides a baseline for negotiation about what new resources will be needed, or what should be postponed in order to accommodate the new priority.

BE AN ORGANIZATION-WIDE SERVICE, NOT A "VOLUNTEER PROGRAM"

Don't isolate your efforts by calling what you do a "volunteer program." That approach (1) implies that you are the owner of volunteer involvement, when in actuality you are providing a service that delivers competent human resources with useful skills to as many areas of the library's work as possible; and (2) also implies that you are the only one responsible for volunteer engagement activities, instead of being the catalyst for engaging volunteers with a variety of staff, in various activities and programs throughout the organization.

And while you're at it, don't call them "my volunteers" for the same reason.

ENGAGE SKILLED VOLUNTEERS

Although you will probably always need volunteer help in the traditional library volunteer positions—shelving, book repair, and shelf-reading—please be sure to take a step beyond that to engage today's skilled volunteers.

Not only will it give you opportunities to reach goals you couldn't otherwise—like expanding a service, enhancing a program, or taking your public relations efforts to a new level—it will attract community members who may not have had a relationship with a library in a long time. The opportunity to enlighten them about today's library while engaging their skills and interests in volunteering has the additional impact of watching them turning into library ambassadors, supporters, and advocates.

GAIN STAFF BUY-IN

Pull out all the stops to get staff on board. Remember that they may have real concerns blocking their support for volunteer engagement. Find out what they are and counteract them:

- Create and get a mission statement approved that clearly states that the role of volunteers is to *supplement* the roles of professional staff, not to supplant them.
- "Pilot test" some skilled volunteer opportunities and share success to help staff get on board.
- Train staff on volunteer engagement best practices to show how bad experiences they've had in the past with volunteers won't be repeated.
- Engage staff in volunteer job description development, interviewing, and training design and delivery to help them develop ownership of volunteer engagement.
- Offer to be available to help if problems arise.

LEAD BY EXAMPLE

Asking staff throughout the library to work with volunteers requires leading by example. You must model it by engaging volunteers in your own work. What things could a skilled volunteer or team of volunteers do to support your work, while at the same time demonstrating successful skilled volunteer engagement?

Could you use someone a few hours a week to do data entry or post volunteer opportunities and respond to interested volunteers in your VolunteerMatch account? Could a volunteer with personnel management skills help with designing interview questions and checking volunteer references? What about a graphic designer to assist with presenting data and results in a meaningful and attractive way?

DEVELOP INTERNAL RELATIONSHIPS

In addition to working closely with the library director, department heads, and members of the volunteer engagement team, it's also important to make a connection with departments that can provide guidance on critical volunteer engagement issues.

Forming a relationship with human resources and risk management administrators, for example, will be helpful in planning strategy and in guiding critical policy details. You'll want to enlist their help for problem solving of course, but consulting with them in advance of a problem arising will not only help to avoid many problems, but will establish a relationship that makes working together to address a problem much more effective.

UTILIZE MULTIPLE RECRUITMENT METHODS

Libraries are notorious for defining recruitment as the posting of a "Volunteer Here" sign on the circulation desk. But if you don't reach out beyond those who already use the library, the opportunity is missed to attract people with skills you need who may not have thought of the library as a place to volunteer.

California's Get Involved data demonstrates that the majority of library volunteers recruited through VolunteerMatch have never volunteered in a library before. Anecdotally, libraries have said they reach more younger and more skilled volunteers through their online recruitment efforts.

Employing a targeted recruitment approach that identifies sources of potential volunteers based on their required skills, and sharing volunteer job openings and skills needed with management, staff, current volunteers, and the board, Friends, and Foundation will encourage them to reach out to their personal and professional contacts who have the skills and interest you're seeking.

MEASURE AND SHARE RESULTS

It's critical to measure the results of your volunteer engagement efforts, and it's not enough to just report the annual number of volunteers and volunteer hours. Quantifying in dollars the impact of volunteers is only the second small step in measuring results.

Share the impact of their work in meaningful ways such as the use of brief anecdotal success stories, return on investment data, and/or full-blown outcome measurement strategies.

Sustaining the volunteer engagement effort will require an ability to share success in meaningful ways so that management and staff continue to be enthusiastic about supporting volunteer engagement efforts. Be sure they're aware of the impact that's being made—create an annual report, speak at staff, board, and community meetings, and provide information to be included in the library's annual report.

DON'T FORGET ABOUT THE LIBRARY SUPPORT GROUPS

Hopefully you've included members of the board, Friends, and Foundation on the volunteer engagement team. Their involvement provides additional input for planning purposes but also provides training for them in how to successfully implement volunteer engagement in their own work.

Your volunteer engagement leadership position may also include some responsibility for recruiting volunteers for, or being the library's liaison to, one or more of these groups. If you don't know what your duties are in this regard, or don't understand the relationship between the library volunteer engagement efforts and those of the board, Friends, and Foundation, it's important that you meet first with the library director for clarification, and then depending on the role you'll be expected to play, meet with the group's leadership to ensure that no toes are stepped on inadvertently.

CHAPTER SUMMARY

There's a lot of information in this book. Remember, you can't do it all at once. Approach it through the eyes of today's volunteer as well as the needs the library has to serve its community, then apply the strategies just summarized and the techniques in this book for the best chance of success.

Wondering where to start? You'll find a call to action and a three-step process for how to get started in the "Epilogue," next.

Epilogue

Let's Get Started! Call to Action

OK, so you've finished reading this book and find yourself feeling energized and overwhelmed at the same time. How can you ever accomplish all this?!

With any big project, it's always helpful to ask yourself: "How does one eat an elephant?" The answer?—one bite at a time.

STEP 1: UNDERSTAND YOUR ROLE

Gain an understanding of your role in this volunteer engagement endeavor: What percentage of your time will be directed to it, what management's goals are for it, and what other resources will be made available to you?

STEP 2: DETERMINE PRIORITIES TO KNOW WHERE TO BEGIN

You should not expect to be able to implement all the volunteer engagement ideas and strategies immediately and in all library departments at once.

Identifying priorities clears the way for knowing where to start. Because you can't do it all at once, knowing the first most important steps to take will jumpstart the planning process and reduce your anxiety.

Define the initial priorities to address by assessing the state of the organization's current volunteer engagement effort.

Presented below in order of intensiveness are three tools for assessment of your library's readiness to begin or expand volunteer engagement. Take a look at all three and determine which suits your current situation and comfort level. You may choose to begin with a less intensive approach, and over time, utilize a more intense version as your efforts grow.

Tool 1: Organizational Readiness Assessment

Take a look at the figure below. This assessment is by far the most basic—it's shorter and less intense than the two that follow—but nevertheless captures the key elements for library success with volunteer engagement. This was designed as a place to begin for those libraries that are just starting out with volunteers, or who have a small number of volunteers in traditional roles, or have a new or inexperienced volunteer engagement staff person assigned.

Assessing Organizational Readiness for Volunteer Engagement in Your Library

Complete the form and rate your library on each of the following factors by circling a number that describes the situation for your library. Is the answer for each closer to TRUE or closer to FALSE? Then determine the three most critical areas to address, and develop an action plan to achieve them.

	True				False
1. Management is supportive of volunteer engagement.	5	4	3	2	1
2. The volunteer engagement coordinator and/or volunteer engagement team have the time, budget, and resources available to do the job effectively.	5	4	3	2	1
3. Volunteer engagement is included in the library's strategic plan, volunteer positions are developed to support strategic plan goals, and the operational plan for volunteer engagement is reviewed and revised at least annually.	5	4	3	2	1
4. Written volunteer job descriptions are designed to be meaningful to the volunteer and include clearly defined roles, qualifications, and benefits.	5	4	3	2	1
5. Volunteer jobs at the library include some that will require high-skilled volunteers in addition to traditional roles.	5	4	3	2	1
6. Staff are supportive of expanding volunteer engagement and have the training needed to carry out their roles.	5	4	3	2	1
7. We have a recruitment plan that includes multiple methods and are making maximum use of the VolunteerMatch tools.	5	4	3	2	1

(*continued*)

	True				False
8. Volunteers are carefully recruited and screened *(interviewed, plus background check, if required)* to ensure a good fit.	5	4	3	2	1
9. Volunteers receive both orientation and training required to successfully do the job assigned.	5	4	3	2	1
10. We have designed volunteer opportunities to ensure sustainability—the work continues if a volunteer moves on.	5	4	3	2	1
11. Our recognition plan is not one-size-fits-all but includes strategies that are meaningful to volunteers.	5	4	3	2	1
12. We have determined how we will measure and share volunteer engagement results.	5	4	3	2	1

Tool 2: Volunteer Program Benchmark Assessment

Developed by the Executive Service Corps of Chicago, the Volunteer Program Benchmark Assessment tool includes a somewhat longer list of items on a checklist segmented out by standards such as Organizational Capacity, Planning, Recruiting and Placing, etc. It also provides the opportunity to identify a "baseline" for each item, which can be reviewed on a regular ongoing basis, suggesting that it be repeated at least every 12 months. You can find the Volunteer Program Benchmark Assessment tool here: https://www.execservicecorps.org/volunteer-benchmark-assessment (accessed October 6, 2017).

Tool 3: Library Volunteer Program Improvement Model

The California State Library and VolunteerMatch developed the Library Volunteer Program Improvement Model as a self-assessment tool for libraries participating in the Get Involved initiative. It is based on the Carnegie Mellon Capability Maturity Model, designed to develop and assess organizational processes. Surveys and pilot testing with California libraries of all sizes informed its definitions, performance levels, indicators, and resources.

This tool assists libraries in assessing their volunteer engagement practices. The goal is to compare what a library is doing against best practices in the field and identify where improvements could be made.

Upon completion of the survey, the tool automatically generates an e-mailed report containing not only the results, but also suggesting resources and strategies to assist with program development in areas where the model identified need for improvement.

In the report, one of five performance levels is calculated for the library based on its responses—from "Ad Hoc," describing a low degree of best practices, to "Optimized," which confirms processes that are effective and sustainable.

A library can move up the levels by implementing best practices and then retaking the survey over time. There's no limit to the number of times it can be taken, so progress can be measured quarterly, annually, or whenever the time is right for each library.

The tool also analyzes your library's status and anonymously compares it with the libraries who have used it. It then makes a second comparison with just similar sized libraries. The Library Volunteer Program Improvement Model can be found here: https://getinvolvedclearinghouse.org/resource/training-materials/library-volunteer-program-improvement-model (accessed February 14, 2018). It is the brainchild of Samir Shah, of VolunteerMatch. Other members of the VolunteerMatch team worked on this as well, including Kevin Johnson and Jennifer Bennett.

STEP 3: LET HUMAN NATURE AND YOUR OWN HUMANITY BE YOUR GUIDE

Whether you lead a big volunteer engagement effort or a small one, paying attention to human needs and interests—whether those of management, board, staff, or volunteers—will help to move things along in the right direction. Here are just a few ways to keep you and others committed to volunteer engagement.

Cheerlead

Be enthusiastic. Thank people for their efforts. Talk and write about success wherever and whenever you have the opportunity.

Engage and Empower People

For most, responsibility for engaging volunteers is only a portion of your job. Engage others—management, staff, volunteers, board members, and Friends—who are willing to take on an assignment and will feel great about being asked.

Recruit members of a volunteer engagement team who are willing to help with research, planning, and implementation tasks they find interesting, have the skills for, or want to learn more about. Then find one or more skilled volunteers to assist with day-to-day tasks associated with the volunteer engagement coordinator's responsibilities.

Recruit your "champions" to play leadership roles. They will feel recognized for their work, honored to be tapped to lead, and will be additional "cheerleading" resources.

Identify potential collaborative partner organizations in the community who could bring their strengths to the table and gain something they need through a partnership with the library.

Communicate Well and Often

Regular, ongoing communication keeps the volunteer engagement strategy in the limelight for busy staff and helps to minimize the impact on staff buy-in when there is staff turnover. Offer periodic in-person updates on process and progress—at full staff meetings, department meetings, and training events. Remember that not everyone learns everything by reading your e-mails.

Be Supportive

Make yourself available to coach, to answer questions, and to problem solve.

SUMMARY

So that's it! This book was intended to serve as a hands-on guidebook for libraries that wish to upgrade their volunteer engagement practices to expand or enhance services, reach out to new customers, and gain new advocates and supporters in their communities.

Hopefully you will use it as a roadmap to help you get started and to guide you along the way. The remaining sections of this book are there to help you locate resources you might need, and to troubleshoot issues or problems that may arise.

Whether or not volunteer engagement is just a piece of your jam-packed workload, or it's your full-time job, whether it's fully funded or barely funded, or whether your library is large or small, the strategies and tactics in this book can be scaled to your available resources.

Take a moment to think about the importance of what you're doing. Not only are you supporting the work of the library and helping it to embed itself deeper into its community, you're also strengthening the voluntary sector, which I believe next to voting, is our most powerful expression of democracy.

And remember that you're not alone! Hopefully you will make use of the many resources available, not the least of which are your colleagues—both in libraries and outside of them—who are passionate about volunteer engagement and who are generally willing to share their ideas, their materials, and their support. You can do this!

Appendix

Troubleshooting

HOW TO USE THIS APPENDIX: There's no law against reading this material now, but here's how it was meant to be used. In a month or a year—whenever you find yourself up against an issue you're not sure how to address—pick up this Appendix and read the section relating to your problem. Each of the sections will also point you to parts of the book where more information can be found to help you with it.

INTRODUCTION

> *"Failure to meet the mark is rarely the fault of the target."*
>
> —*Unknown*

That's one of my favorite quotes. I don't share it so the volunteer engagement coordinator feels like he or she must be blamed for every problem that arises. It's just a reminder that when problems do arise, the "target"—volunteer, staff, supervisor, or library director—may not be the only cause. Look more closely at the situation to see what might have been missed if you're not getting the results you hoped for.

Volunteers don't step forward to make you miserable. Staff and management don't come to work in the morning with the goal of resisting volunteer engagement, but they may have legitimate concerns or fears that must be addressed before they're willing to buy in.

This Appendix uses the tools and strategies discussed in this book to help you prevent, address, and even solve some of the common frustrations faced in the implementation or expansion of volunteer engagement efforts at the library.

THE BIG FOUR

I've found these four to be the most commonly asked about problem areas—staff buy-in, union issues, where will I find the time, and firing a volunteer—so let's get them out of the way first.

The Staff Are Not Supportive: How Do We Get Them to Buy In?

Staff may be afraid that an increase in volunteers means a loss of staff positions or may have past negative experiences that make them cringe at the thought of working with volunteers. Give them an opportunity to share their concerns, invite them to participate in crafting the plan, shine a light on volunteer successes, train them in good volunteer engagement practices, and demonstrate how both they and the library can do more for the community with the help of volunteers.

Allay their fears about their jobs being replaced with volunteers by creating a mission statement stressing that volunteers *supplement* and don't supplant the work of staff.

Once they know their jobs are not at risk, staff's feelings of ownership of volunteer engagement come next from an understanding about what the goal of volunteer engagement is—not only getting the usual work done but reaching out to new potential library supporters and advocates that have skills to share. Hearing the library director say that is the most potent form of communicating it.

Find your staff champions, pilot test some volunteer engagement projects with them and then share results. Another powerful motive for staff to come on board is to see that skilled volunteers can help with expanding or maintaining a project, allowing staff to spend time on new ideas or projects that have been waiting for their attention.

Ownership by staff is further fostered by enlisting them to help with design of job descriptions and training programs you'll be using for volunteers in their area of the library.

The ongoing message to staff needs to be: this is big, and it's not going away. Engaging volunteers is an important strategy the library will use to both serve and connect with the community—we'll train you to do it well, and we'll be here to help.

Where to find more help in this book: Chapter 1, "Developing a Volunteer Engagement Mission Statement" and sample statements (appendices) (pp. 5, 11, 13), and Chapter 5, "Success Factor 5: Staff Buy-In" (p. 77).

Our Union Won't Allow Us to Use Volunteers

This issue may be a perception rather than a reality. In our work with California libraries—which are mostly unionized—interviews with a number of library directors about their union contracts found that none had specific language on the use—or nonuse—of volunteers. Most directors interviewed shared that they had discussed the issue with union leadership and had at least an "unwritten agreement" with the union that volunteers would not supplant employees. We found only one library whose union had forbidden volunteers to do shelving because they were concerned about the staff page positions.

During the California State Library's implementation of skilled volunteer engagement, the human resources director agreed to review all of our volunteer job descriptions and talk with the union if necessary, before approving them for recruitment to ensure that no staff position would be supplanted by the work of volunteers.

Begin this discussion with a review of your library's collective bargaining agreement, and then have a conversation with the library director to determine your local reality. Then, it's best to have the library director bring a union representative into the discussions about implementing or expanding a volunteer engagement initiative, to keep them apprised of planning and progress, and to have their input into the planning—even offer a seat on the volunteer engagement team to a union representative.

A key strategy to avoid problems in this area is to establish a mission statement for volunteer engagement that specifically states that volunteers will supplement, not supplant the work of library staff.

Where to find more help in this book: Chapter 1, "What Will Get in Your Way? Union Issues and Staff Resistance" (p. 4) and "Developing a Volunteer Engagement Mission Statement" and sample statements (appendices) (pp. 5, 11, 13).

I Don't Have Enough Time for This!

You've read the book, so you know there are a lot of things to do to be successful with volunteer engagement, and since many library volunteer engagement coordinators are not full-time in that role, you may be feeling overwhelmed about how it will all get done.

The good news is that not all of it must be done by you—nor should it be. To ensure organizational commitment and staff ownership of volunteer engagement, there's an important role for almost everyone in the library to play.

Start with gaining a very clear understanding of what's being asked of the volunteer engagement coordinator: What are the library director's goals for this initiative? If you're not full-time, what is the specific percentage of your work time that can be dedicated to volunteer engagement? What other resources have been assigned to this besides a portion of your time? Is it focused strictly on volunteer engagement within the library, or will working with Friends of the Library or a library foundation be part of the assignment?

Once you have the big picture, if there's no job description for the volunteer engagement leader, write one. Meet with your supervisor and the library director to share the draft job description to help them understand what it takes to do this job effectively. They must be crystal clear on the fact that it's not enough to just say "Get a volunteer to do it!"

Now, get yourself some help. Design skilled volunteer positions to work directly with you on volunteer engagement tasks. Could you use someone to help manage your VolunteerMatch account? Someone with data entry, event management, or photography skills? Or someone to design flyers or format your annual report? This approach not only helps with your time management, but demonstrates to staff that you're not just asking them to work with volunteers—you're willing to do it as well. Being a role model in this area will not only help you but will assist with staff buy-in.

Delegating effectively will empower other staff and volunteers to help. This can provide promotional opportunities for volunteers who can serve as project leaders or advisers, as well as opportunities for staff to provide their input, share their skills, and gain ownership of the process.

Share volunteer engagement success stories with management in addition to actual data about results to make a case that more of your time, and/or other staff's time as well as additional resources are both needed and justified.

Be a planner. Identify ways that volunteers can assist in achieving organizational strategic goals, and get them included in the library's strategic plan, along with overall volunteer engagement goals and objectives. Together with the volunteer engagement team, create an operational plan for volunteer engagement. Based on both strategic plan goals and volunteer engagement best practices, what should be the operational goals for this year? Next year?

Having a plan allows the delineation of priorities. Focusing on priorities provides an unobstructed path to implementation and resists the temptation to do it all right now or be all things to all people.

A written plan that's been approved by management also provides the luxury of negotiation when a new project materializes midyear: Which project takes precedence over what was agreed to for this year? Or could it all be done if additional resources were made available?

Up your personal game by taking a class in time management or project management and practicing self-preservation by scheduling out your time, even creating "office hours," or hiding for short periods to get something done in a place that makes you less immediately available if necessary. There also exist a plethora of time management and project management tools that might be helpful. Talk to others about what they use, or a quick Google search on either term will supply ideas to investigate.

And finally, read a great book on this very subject by Katherine Noyes Campbell and Susan J. Ellis.[1]

Where to find more help in this book: Chapter 6, "Considerations for Volunteer Engagement Leaders" (p. 97) and "Avoiding Burn-Out of the Volunteer Engagement Coordinator" (p. 101), Chapter 7, "Measuring Success" (p. 126), and Chapter 8, "Plan, Plan, Plan" (p. 137).

Can I Fire a Volunteer?

When I first got started working on volunteerism with libraries, I did a training needs assessment survey and was astounded when so many responses said that one of the top issues they wanted covered in the training was "how to fire a volunteer."

This wasn't astounding because volunteers can't be fired—of course they can. I was surprised that this manifested the amount of work that needed to be done with libraries on volunteer engagement!

Here's the deal—use the strategies and tactics in this book as a way to prevent problems. By designing a meaningful volunteer job with clear expectations, and then carefully selecting the right person—you avoid the vast majority of problems that may occur, and may never have to fire one.

Be sure that volunteers understand what to expect, give them a meaningful role that they have the required skills for, and if it meets their personal motivation for volunteering, most of the concerns you have won't materialize.

In the interview, make sure you're not talking someone into taking a position he or she doesn't want—be sure to give the person the opportunity to say no, thus preventing a future problem.

If it's not working, find out why not. They volunteer to be helpful. Identify the cause and fix the problem:

- Have you been clear enough about expectations?
- Are they in the wrong job? Were they asked enough questions, or did they just tell you what they thought you wanted to hear, instead of what they really felt?
- Is there a personality conflict with a staff member or other volunteer? If so, can you intervene or place them with a different person or in a different job? (*Note*: If there's a persistent issue with getting along with others, it may be time to help the volunteer to move on.)

- Are they overcommitted and don't know how to tell you? Sometimes reliable people commit and then don't show up—has something in their life changed since they committed?—perhaps an unanticipated job change, extra work stress, sick family member, or divorce?

This person is dying for you to let them off the hook, and the reason they don't call is because they feel guilty for not following through. When you call, they say, "I'm so glad you called, I've been meaning to call you. I'm overcommitted, I can't do what I said I would do, I feel terrible." Isn't that better?—to know, instead of wonder? To give them a way out? They won't be mad, they'll be relieved. Warm person-to-person outreach is the key: "Are you in farther than you want to be? Can I help you?" In most cases, that will take care of it. You might lose them temporarily, but they will be loyal to you because of what you did for them and will probably come back when their issue is resolved and time permits.

Where to find more help in this book: Chapter 3, "Motivation" (p. 35) and "Designing Good Volunteer Job Descriptions" (p. 38), and Chapter 5, "Success Factor 6: Feedback, Collaboration, and Support" (p. 80).

Alternatives to Firing

If a volunteer is not meeting expectations and your coaching efforts don't work, is firing this person the only option? No, not if you can make a better fit for them in another job, either at the library or in another organization: "Jane, you seem frustrated in this role, and I want you to be happy. Tell me how I can help. . . . Why don't we take a look at what other things need to get done around here, and see if we can find something that's a better fit for you."

REAL-LIFE EXAMPLE:
ALTERNATIVE TO FIRING

Once I was working with the volunteer chair of a key committee who was just not demonstrating the leadership skills required to be successful in that position. He was a long-time, very committed volunteer, who had served on the committee for several years before being tapped to be its vice chair.

Unfortunately, his enthusiasm for and knowledge of the committee's subject area had masked his lack of leadership skills, until he was promoted to serve as chair of the committee.

The committee was floundering, and other members were frustrated, so it was clear that something had to be done. Instead of embarrassing this loyal volunteer with a demotion, however, we were able to find a suitable lateral transfer that would solve the committee problem and allow him to save face.

A very specific problem had arisen in the community on a topic of importance to the organization. Because he had a strong history with the organization's needs and interests and was well versed in its mission and policies, we were able to ask him to sacrifice his committee chairmanship in order to take on a role as leader of a task force to address the issue. Because the position would have staff working more closely with him, it made his lack of leadership skills a less serious issue and would utilize his skills and expertise on the subject to solve an important problem.

Talk to the individual about other suitable volunteer positions at the library that they could transfer into. If you don't have one, say so. Or if those you offer are not of interest to the volunteer, ask if they would like you to call the Volunteer Center or show them how to use VolunteerMatch to see what opportunities outside the library might be available. Express your thanks for their time and for their interest in being involved and that you hope the community won't lose their enthusiasm to volunteer.

Firing a Volunteer

Sometimes you have to fire somebody, however. If someone crosses the line on safety or confidentiality, is inappropriate with a patron, or misrepresents the library, there's a risk to the library of maintaining that relationship.

A good prevention technique is to identify "Grounds for Termination" right in the volunteer job description. If the role will include maintaining confidentiality, include "Grounds for Termination: Breaking Confidentiality" on the job description, and bring to potential volunteers' attention during interviews, orientation, and training the importance of maintaining confidentiality.

Don't take action by yourself, and don't rely on secondhand information alone. Work with the human resources staff in your library (or city or county) or with your library director to corroborate the information, and together sit down with and confront the volunteer.

From the 2013 Charity Lawyer blog: "Dismissal of Volunteers . . . be ready and willing to dismiss a volunteer if necessary. Volunteers should be held to a high standard. Here are some tips on handling the dismissal of a volunteer:

- If appropriate, have a meeting with the volunteer to address concerns and possible remedies
- Have a formal, written process in place to remove volunteers
- Document the removal of the volunteer"[2]

Establishing a good relationship with human resources—hopefully before there's a problem—is critical if and when a volunteer commits a fireable offense.

In some situations, human resources or your library director may also wish to involve the library's legal counsel and/or risk manager, who may also be part of your city or county government.

Something else that's risked by not acting on a serious problem is support of the other volunteers: "Why does he get away with that?" And if the staff observe nonaction on a serious problem, their response will be: "See, I knew it, she won't do anything about it—quality is going to go down. I told you so!"

REAL-LIFE EXAMPLE: FIRING A VOLUNTEER

In all my years of working with volunteers, I had to fire a volunteer only one time—a volunteer in a "train-the-trainer" session. His practice presentation during the training session clearly determined that he would not be a good representative of the organization. We explained to him privately afterward that we would not be able to certify him to serve as one of our trainers. He was unhappy. After all, he had just given up his weekend to be trained for this volunteer position.

Did we risk having him speak negatively in the community about the program and our organization? Yes. But a greater concern would have been allowing him to represent the organization poorly.

Fortunately, we had included in the trainer job description that trainees would need to be certified following the weekend training and had stressed that both in the interviews and in the orientation. So even though he was angry, it wasn't a surprise that we had the prerogative to take that step.

Where to find more help in this book: Chapter 5, "Interviewing" (p. 70), and Chapter 7, "Liability and Risk Management" (p. 119).

MOTIVATION-RELATED ISSUES

Problems almost always arise when volunteers are not a good fit for the job they've been given. Either they don't have the skills for it, it doesn't relate to their motivation for volunteering, or it just doesn't interest them.

Volunteer Absenteeism

Begin by asking yourself if the assignment serves an important purpose. Is it meaningful? Does it make any difference if it's completed or not? What impact is made if a volunteer contributes his or her time to it? If you don't have answers, the volunteer certainly won't be able to. Look here for the basis of the problem.

Perhaps there's not a good fit between the volunteer and the job. Is it meeting *their* motivation for being there? Do they have the right skills to be successful? Was the training program sufficient, or do they feel unprepared? You need to talk to the volunteer to find out. If a poor match has been made, you need to offer another assignment.

Remember that rather than have the wrong volunteer in the position, you're better off with a vacancy.

Unfortunately, there remains a perspective out in the world that volunteers should just do what needs to be done and not presume to ask for something that meets their skills and interests. If that's their perspective, they don't know how to tell you they're not happy, so they don't—they just disappear. You owe it to them—and to yourself—to give them a call.

You also owe it to your volunteer engagement efforts to resolve the issue. Not addressing absenteeism can generate a morale problem—other volunteers and staff will notice that you're not making this volunteer accountable. Some staff will go back to their old thought pattern—that volunteers can't meet expectations—and other volunteers might decide that missing a day or not meeting a deadline is no big deal.

Where to find more help in this book: Chapter 3, "Motivation" (p. 35) and "Designing Good Volunteer Job Descriptions" (p. 38), and Chapter 4, "What If They Say No?" (p. 65).

The Volunteer Doesn't Return after the First Week

This volunteer either doesn't want the job you assigned them, or is having a life crisis. Call them.

The Volunteer Isn't Doing the Job Right

A volunteer will be so embarrassed if you let this go on. Thinking that others know or will find out that they're doing the job incorrectly will be mortifying. Check in with this volunteer and do a little coaching: "You're doing a great job on the first aspect of the assignment, but did you understand this second part during the training? Maybe I can explain it a little better while I show you." Or ask a long-time volunteer to do a little mentoring. After that, if the volunteer still doesn't get it, or doesn't like it, offer the person a different role. The volunteer is most likely frustrated with the experience as well.

Volunteers Only Want to Do What They Want to Do

Correct! They didn't volunteer to participate in something they don't like or don't have the skills for! If you're still offering potential volunteers only the traditional volunteer assignments, or worse yet, just asking them to sign up to be a "library volunteer"—to come in and do a shift of whatever you need done that day—you're not addressing the needs and interests of today's volunteer.

So, will the traditional, "nonglamorous" volunteer jobs be left vacant? Of course not! People have varying interests and skills for volunteering—while some prefer a repetitive job, others will want a challenge. Your superpower needs to be ensuring the right "fit" for each job and each volunteer.

Where to find more help in this book: Chapter 2, "Trend 1: Generational Differences" (p. 15), "Trend 2: Skilled Volunteers" (p. 19), and "Trend 3: Shift from Volunteer Management to Volunteer Engagement" (p. 20), and Chapter 3, "Why People Volunteer" (p. 35).

When Someone Brings His or Her Own Idea

You already have plenty to do. Even if the concept a volunteer brings to you sounds wonderful—like starting a homebound delivery service or a maker space—remember that it will require your time, as well as some resources.

If it will create more work for you, don't take on even a great idea, unless it's a priority for the library, *and* you—or your supervisor—can adjust not only your workload but also any other required resources to accommodate it. Be up front with the volunteer in this situation. Thank him or her profusely, but explain the limitations—the staff time can't accommodate it and the budgetary realities can't support it.

If it's a project you think you'd like to try, and you're sure the volunteer has the requisite planning and organizational skills needed, explain several other projects are already waiting, but if the volunteer really wants to pursue it, you're willing to consider taking some initial steps.

Propose the possibility of planning for a pilot project with an end date—being sure to identify the realities of minimal staff time and limited resources that could be given to it. Involve the volunteer in designing the project, and plan to evaluate the pilot phase to determine if it's making an impact and if there's a feasible plan to proceed before making the decision to continue.

Both you and the volunteer must be clear that you don't want to create high expectations for the community that can't be met on a continuous basis, so that in the program planning, a mechanism must be designed to continue it with volunteers. "I'm very supportive of this, it's a great idea, but let's be sure we can plan for its continuation because there isn't funding for library staffing of this project on an ongoing basis."

Where to find more help in this book: Chapter 5, "Collaborating with and Supporting Skilled Volunteers" (p. 81).

RECRUITMENT ISSUES

Potential volunteers with all kinds of skills are everywhere. But using the traditional "Volunteer Here" sign on the circulation desk and waiting for them to walk through the door and present themselves won't work very well. Finding the right volunteer for the right job is critical to success with skilled volunteers. Using targeted, rather than passive, recruitment is the key.

How Does One Recruit Skilled Volunteers?

First, design a meaningful written volunteer job description that defines the skills required for the position. Then use the Targeted Recruitment Plan in the Appendix for Chapter 4, "Volunteer Recruitment." Lay it down next to the job description for the position you're seeking a skilled volunteer for, and fill in the blanks—hopefully together with a couple of people you can brainstorm with.

You've already laid out the qualifications needed and benefits that will accrue to this volunteer in the job description. Now ask yourself how to locate someone who has those skills. Do people like this congregate anywhere? What contacts do members of your team have that might yield the perfect person? And who should do the asking?

If the library director, staff, board, and other volunteers aren't aware of the skilled volunteers you're seeking, they can't help you find them. Be sure to share recruitment needs with them, and when the perfect potential volunteer is identified, determine who is the best person to ask them. If it would help, go along with that person to help close the deal.

Targeted recruitment turns your effort into a heat-seeking missile, rather than a passive bystander waiting for the right people to walk into the library and reveal themselves.

Online recruitment is another path for recruitment of skilled volunteers and reaches out beyond who you and other library supporters might know. On VolunteerMatch, for example, volunteers have an advanced search option that allows them to search by skills they wish to share. In addition, when you post a volunteer opportunity on VolunteerMatch, and select at least one skill from the taxonomy of skills embedded there, both VolunteerMatch and LinkedIn will begin to share the opportunity with nearby volunteers who have identified that they have those skills and are willing to share them.

Where to find more help in this book: Chapter 2, "Trend 4: Corporate Volunteerism" (p. 22), and Chapter 4, "Online Recruitment" (p. 61).

How Does One Go about Finding Virtual Volunteers?

Start by thinking of jobs you need done that can be done by someone not in your office—graphic design, research, writing, translating documents, or even grant writing, like the skilled grant writer in North Carolina who is volunteering for a library in a town she's never been to in far off Idaho.

Those opportunities can be posted on VolunteerMatch and marked "virtual" rather than "one location." Then volunteers can search for a virtual opportunity on VolunteerMatch's home page—one tab is marked "Local" and the other "Virtual."

Where to find more help in this book: Chapter 2, "Real-Life Example: Virtual Volunteer" (p. 25) and "Real-Life Example: Where the Need for Social Media Assistance, Online Recruiting, Virtual Volunteering, and Online Meeting Technology Converged" (p. 28).

Can I Say No to a Potential Volunteer?

Yes, and you *should* if the person is not a good fit.

You also want to give the volunteer a chance to say no before, during, or after the interview. Just a reminder that a vacancy is better than the wrong volunteer.

Where to find more help in this book: Chapter 4, "What If They Say No?" (p. 65), and Chapter 5, "Saying No to a Volunteer after the Interview" (p. 73).

I'm Not Getting the Results from VolunteerMatch I Was Hoping for: What Can I Do?

Most often I find that people who aren't getting the results they had hoped for on VolunteerMatch are making one of these mistakes:

- Not using the VolunteerMatch tools that are available to ensure your postings get the most visibility, such as using a photo of what it looks like to be the volunteer, and the repost feature, which brings the opportunity back up to the first page of the search results, among others.
- Not describing the volunteer opportunity clearly enough so that a potential volunteer understands what the job entails, what skills or other qualifications are required, and how much time is expected. Copy and paste enough of the volunteer job description you've created for the position into VolunteerMatch. Be sure what you post clearly describes enough information to answer the volunteers' initial questions and get them to click on the "I Want to Help" button.

Where to find more help in this book: Chapter 3, "Designing Good Volunteer Job Descriptions" (p. 38), and Chapter 4, "Online Recruitment with VolunteerMatch.org" (p. 61).

LIBRARY DIRECTOR AND MANAGEMENT SUPPORT ISSUES

Your volunteer engagement efforts will be most successful if you have commitment from the top—from the library director and the management team. The director must be visible and vocal about the importance of engaging volunteers for the library, not just to get work done, but to reach out to community members who can also evolve into library supporters, ambassadors, and advocates.

If the director doesn't prioritize it or if their supervisor doesn't support it, staff won't think it's important.

Where to find more help in this book: Chapter 6, "Roles for the Library Director" (p. 94), and Chapter 6 (appendix), "Matrix: Roles in Volunteer Engagement" (p. 108).

Our Volunteer Services Department Is an Afterthought at Our Library

If you're the only person that ever talks about volunteer engagement or brings it up in staff meetings, you must take steps to see that it is elevated to a higher standing in the library. A key player in making that happen is the library director.

The director can absolutely set the tone by including discussions of volunteer engagement in staff meetings—why it's important, what we hope to gain from it, and that everyone in the organization plays a role in making it a success.

Some additional powerful ways the library director can make a statement are:

- Includes volunteer engagement goals in the library's strategic plan.
- Position volunteer engagement as an organization-wide service rather than a separate program.
- Place it high enough in the organization to allow the volunteer engagement leader regular access to management staff and projects.
- Assign volunteer(s) to work with the director, such as a skilled volunteer in strategic planning or public relations, so the director leads by example.

Each of these demonstrates to staff that volunteer engagement is a high priority for the library.

Another way you can help to raise the level of awareness and support for volunteer engagement by the director, management, and staff is to measure and share results of your work. If you're only reporting numbers of volunteers and hours served, you're bound to be asked "So, what?" Consider adding success stories, return on investment calculations, and/or outcome measures to your reporting to really "wow" them.

Where to find more help in this book: Chapter 6, "Roles for the Library Director" (p. 94), "Placement of Volunteer Engagement in the Library's Structure" (p. 97), and "Helping Staff to Understand Your Role" (p. 99), and Chapter 7, "Measuring Success" (p. 126).

How Can I Get My Manager to Accept This?

So, you've just finished the book and you want to propose implementation (or expansion) of skilled volunteer engagement to your boss. What should you do?

Start with a list of all the things you found exciting in this book—places where you said, "That's a great idea!" Or, "That would be such a help to us!" You'll be able to be more persuasive when talking about an idea you're enthusiastic about.

If you thought of a staff "champion" while you were reading—perhaps someone who sees the need to offer more computer assistance to seniors, or a program coordinator who could use some graphic design or public relations help, or someone who's been tasked with implementing a goal from the library's strategic plan. Share some of what you've learned with them, and if they get excited too, engage them in creating a plan for a pilot project utilizing skilled volunteers to assist.

Then, take your excitement and your proposal for a pilot project to your supervisor, and get him or her excited about it too. You'll likely be asked how much of your time (and your champion's time) this will take, and what other resources will be needed to carry it off, so you should also have the beginnings of an operational plan ready to address at least those questions.

During the meeting, gather your supervisor's additional concerns and questions, and offer to come back with the answers to them together with a plan that includes realistic goals and timelines for achieving them. Follow through is key, so schedule that next meeting before the first one ends.

If your supervisor—or theirs—needs additional motivation or has more questions, kick in to training mode by:

- sharing this book with specific sections marked that address their issues or concerns;

- sharing video clips or archived webinars that support your enthusiasm for volunteer engagement;[3] and
- arranging a meeting for yourself and your boss with another nearby library volunteer engagement leader and their boss who can demonstrate success.

Here's a list of potential "sales pitch" topics that might be helpful for use with your supervisor depending on issues or concerns raised in your library:

- California's Get Involved research shows that a huge majority of these new volunteers have never volunteered in a library before, demonstrating that this approach brings new community members to the library, and that in addition to sharing skills to address the library's mission, they naturally develop into community ambassadors, as well as library supporters and advocates. (Read more in the Preface to this book.)
- Techniques for overcoming staff resistance and gaining their buy-in for volunteer engagement.
- Ideas for measuring results beyond counting the numbers of volunteers and hours—return on investment perhaps?
- An idea for volunteer engagement that will get the library to completion of a strategic goal.

Where to find more help in this book: Preface, "Why This Could Work for You" (p. xv), Chapter 5, "Success Factor 5: Staff Buy-In" (p. 77), Chapter 6, "The Roles of Staff in Volunteer Engagement" (p. 105), and Chapter 7, "Measuring Success" (p. 126).

How Can I Make the Case That I Need More Resources?

Showcase success stories. Demonstrate results. Have you been able to address an issue with volunteers that enhanced, expanded, or improved service delivery? Are staff enthusiastic about a problem you helped to solve with volunteers? Did you assist the library to achieve a strategic plan goal through the use of volunteers?

Measure things beyond just the number of volunteers and hours. At least share anecdotal success stories, and try calculating the return on investment for volunteer engagement at your library. Consider going beyond that to demonstrate outcomes.

Where to find more help in this book: Chapter 7, "Measuring Success" (p. 126).

No Funds for a Full-Time Volunteer Engagement Coordinator?

It's certainly not required that an organization begin with a full-time volunteer engagement leader. Starting out with someone assigned part-time, however, means that you can't expect full-time results.

This staff member must focus on all eight of the success factors outlined in Chapter 5, so the number of hours the person has been given will either limit or expand the number of issues that can be successfully addressed with volunteers. Take a look at the sample volunteer engagement coordinator job description and matrix of roles in volunteer engagement in the Appendices for Chapter 6 if you're not convinced this is a professional role for a staff member to play.

Over time, results of volunteer engagement can be analyzed to consider increasing the part-time person's hours in order to expand.

What about a Volunteer as Volunteer Engagement Coordinator?

At this point in the conversation, someone usually asks, "What about using a volunteer as volunteer engagement coordinator?" I don't recommend it for a number of reasons—spoiler alert, it's not because I look down on the gifts volunteers bring to the library. You'll find my reasons not to go this route outlined in the section "A Word about Utilizing a Volunteer as Volunteer Engagement Coordinator" in Chapter 6.

OTHER MANAGEMENT AND ADMINISTRATIVE ISSUES

Other issues may be on your mind. Here are a few of those most commonly asked about.

Keeping Track of Volunteer Data

A new volunteer engagement effort can track most of what it needs to know about its volunteers and the services they provide on a spreadsheet, or even in paper files. Over time, however, the activities and number of volunteers involved may expand to the point that the tracking spreadsheet isn't enough.

A number of volunteer management systems (VMS) designed to track information about volunteers and generate reports are available in the marketplace. Many offer a free trial period, and pricing is generally based on the number of volunteers being tracked.

Begin by determining what features are important for your efforts now, based on the number of volunteers you have currently and the reports you wish to generate, and which features might be important in the future as volunteer engagement grows. Reread the "Data Management" section of

Chapter 7, "Administrative and Legal Issues," to help with thinking about the various features that are available, how to decide which ones you need, and for suggestions on additional resources to help with your research.

Comparing notes with volunteer engagement colleagues in other organizations, including libraries, will also help you gather information before making this important decision.

Liability Issues

Although there are federal and state laws that protect volunteers from some liability, they are not protected if they are negligent or reckless or if they are guilty of willful misconduct. And there is no law that protects the organization itself.

Therefore, the importance of internal protective measures—policies, procedures, and insurance—cannot be overstated. Learn about and implement risk assessment, risk avoidance, and risk management principles to protect volunteers, staff, patrons, and the library itself.

Potential liability is a very important discussion to have, but don't find yourself and your library hog-tied by a fear of risk. Become informed on the subject. Connect with key local resources that can advise you—your human resources, risk management and legal experts in your library, your city, or your county. Those relationships can help design risk management practices and will be invaluable later if a problem does arise.

Where to find more help in this book: Chapter 7, "Liability and Risk Management" (p. 119).

How Do We Know If We've Been Successful?

Sharing volunteer engagement success is an important way to justify to management your need for additional resources; to gain enthusiasm and buy-in from staff; and to make volunteers aware of their significant contributions.

Determine what to measure based on what's meaningful in your situation and what you can realistically gather data on. The most basic results you can measure are how many volunteers are engaged and how many hours they've served. Although that data is helpful in determining whether or not volunteer engagement is growing, it doesn't describe actual results of their work and may cause people to think "So what?"

Take additional measurement steps to determine success. From gathering and sharing anecdotal success stories, to calculating return on investment (ROI), to measuring actual outcomes of the work that's being done, there's much more you can do to find out whether your efforts are worth it.

Another key success measure is documenting progress on goals—those goals from the library's strategic plan to which volunteer resources are being applied, and goals in your operational plan for volunteer engagement.

Where to find more help in this book: Chapter 7, "Measuring Success" (p. 126).

We Have Low Attendance at Our Annual Volunteer Recognition Brunch: Why Don't Volunteers Want to Be Thanked?

Low attendance doesn't necessarily equate to volunteers not wanting to be thanked—it may just not be the way they prefer to be thanked. Recognition preferences are one of the trends that requires us to retool our volunteer engagement practices to meet the needs and interests of "today's volunteer."

A 2013 study on volunteer recognition preferences found that volunteers' least preferred ways to be recognized were banquets, formal gatherings, and public acknowledgment, while 80 percent prefer to hear about how their work has made a difference.[4]

Find new ways to acknowledge volunteers that are meaningful to them—such as the opportunity to share skills or gain new ones, the chance to participate in special opportunities, and "career-pathing."

Where to find more help in this book: Chapter 5, "Success Factor 7: Recognition/Acknowledgment" (p. 82).

I Need Training in Volunteer Engagement and Don't Have the Funds

If your library has placed a priority on starting or expanding volunteer engagement, and there is no expertise on staff, consideration should be given in the budget for some training and/or consulting opportunities.

There are books and organizations, websites and listservs, online training opportunities (some free and some at a cost), as well as online certificate programs that can help. Review the Resources section of this book for more information.

Here's one more idea: Have you been a volunteer? If not, get some experience. Of course we should "practice what we preach," but because it's also a terrific training ground for those working on volunteer engagement. You'll get a chance to see the good, the bad, and the ugly "up close and personal."

Volunteering yourself allows you see firsthand what's good and what's bad, what helps and what doesn't, which you might not understand when you lead volunteer engagement. Some key volunteer engagement lessons are learned while volunteering yourself.

RETENTION (SUSTAINABILITY) ISSUES

The volunteer engagement concept of "sustainability" replaces the old volunteer management concept of "retention." In the past, our goal was to keep each volunteer for as many years as we possibly could. Today's volunteer's goal isn't necessarily to stay with a given assignment, or even a given organization, for that long, although, of course, some will.

It's up to the volunteer engagement coordinator to build in sustainability strategies that will allow the work to continue when the volunteer moves on.

Handling the Departure of a Key Volunteer

Unfortunately, the burden of continuing the work of a departing key volunteer will probably fall on the volunteer engagement coordinator, so as soon as you know they're leaving, start the recruitment for that person's replacement.

A better, more preventative approach, however, is to not rely on any individual volunteer so heavily that it causes a crisis when that person has a new baby, gets a promotion at work, or must unexpectedly provide care for a relative.

So, instead of waiting for it to happen, start to think about the possibilities now. Is there a way to have a big job handled by a pair of job-sharing volunteers? Or a team who breaks the assignment down into smaller parts that suit their needs, expertise, and time availability? Consider substitute volunteers or a skilled volunteer who could play the role of volunteer "consultant."

Always have a Plan B for any key volunteer position—a volunteer "in training" for each key position so that you're not left empty-handed. You'll want the task or service to continue when a key volunteer moves on—and he or she wants that, as well. This concept is called "two-deep leadership."

Where to find more help in this book: Chapter 5, "Success Factor 8: Sustainability Strategies" (p. 86).

I Can No Longer Get Volunteers to Take One of Our Most Important Jobs, and It's Critical to Our Operation: What Can I Do?

Today's volunteers don't necessarily want a huge job they can take on and do for the rest of their lives. When you're having trouble filling a big job, consider a new approach to it, such as breaking it into smaller pieces and recruiting a team of two or three volunteers to work on it, instead of having to rely on just one person to do the whole thing.

This approach also enhances sustainability—maintaining the work when a volunteer leaves—because when one of the team volunteers leaves, two remain who continue to handle their part of the assignment, and the volunteer engagement coordinator is not left "holding the bag" for the entire task while working to fill the departing team member's position.

You can watch Monrovia Public Library's Volunteer Management Team describing their work and sharing their strategies and tips.[5]

Where to find more help in this book: Chapter 3, "Job Description Tips" (p. 43), and Chapter 5, "Success Factor 8: Sustainability Strategies" (p. 86).

SPECIAL GROUPS OF VOLUNTEERS

Court-Appointed Volunteers

Volunteers referred to you by the courts would rather serve their time volunteering at the library than in jail. They're really not doing it because they want to, so if they're unreliable or they're making things harder for you rather than helping, talk to the person or organization that made the referral.

Explain that you don't have enough staff to accept volunteers that only create more work. Be clear if that organization can't do better selection of volunteers, and supervise those they send, that the library will be unable to participate.

The organization making those referrals can be successful only if they have placement locations to which they may refer volunteers. If some of the volunteers they send are useful to you, attempt to restructure the way they work with you, rather than severing the entire relationship—just remember that if it makes more work without receiving at least as much benefit, it's not worth continuing.

Youth Volunteers

If you're having issues with young volunteers, address them the same way you would if they were adults: Have we created meaningful assignments for them? Are they clear on what the job is and requires, as well as expectations you have? Did you orient and train them well enough?

Try looking at it from the teens' perspective and ask for guidance—from them! Do some interviews with some young volunteers, and hold a "focus group" to see what their needs and interests are. Then involve them in redesigning youth volunteerism at the library based on what you learn.

If working with teens is not your strength, find someone who's good at it, pick his or her brain, and engage that person as a leader. Start with the children's or teen librarian to see if you can get him or her on board.

More teen volunteer resources can be found in the Get Involved Clearinghouse,[6] and in Young Adult Library Services Association's (YALSA) wiki.[7]

Where to find more help in this book: Chapter 2, "Millennials" (p. 17).

Volunteers with Disabilities

ASCLA, the Association of Specialized and Cooperative Library Agencies, suggests in one of its tip sheets[8]: "The library and community as a whole benefit when the library staff welcome volunteers with disabilities. Individuals with disabilities have many of the same motivations as volunteers without disabilities: Wanting to give back, build a resume, meet a community service requirement for graduation or an organization, or just fill the hours in a day." To that list of potential volunteer motivations I would add "share a skill."

Developing opportunities for people with disabilities to volunteer is an important task in volunteer engagement. As ASCLA[9] reminds us: "be aware that people with disabilities do not necessarily have the same opportunities to volunteer because of intentional or unintentional community barriers."

ASCLA has also developed tip sheets that can help with understanding a variety of different disabilities, including autism spectrum disorders, deaf and hard of hearing, mobility impairments, and mental health issues.[10]

You can help volunteers with disabilities meet their goals for community involvement while getting important work done for the library. Whether your volunteer opportunities are skilled positions or not, whether they are located in the library or can be done by virtual volunteers, making them available to people with disabilities can meet your needs and theirs.

"The volunteering sector can be a powerful setting for promoting inclusion. By supporting and providing opportunities for people who experience exclusion, volunteering can assist them to participate more fully in their community. Volunteering allows individuals who may have traditionally been service users to become service providers. Empowering individuals through volunteering can have an immeasurably positive impact for someone, giving them confidence, satisfaction and community connection."[11]

For more help on inclusive practices, see "Inclusive Volunteering: Recommendations for Volunteer Coordinators on How to Develop a More Inclusive Volunteer Programme."[12]

Friends of the Library

In her July 2017 webinar, "Working with Friends Groups: The Good, the Great, and the Unfriendly,"[13] Sally Gardner Reed shared the origins of Friends of the Library. When Andrew Carnegie offered grants for library buildings only, local groups organized to raise funds for books and staffing. These mostly women's groups also found the need to advocate with their city governments, as Carnegie required the city to fund a minimum of 10 percent of the operational costs of the library in perpetuity.

Today, Friends of the Library continue to raise funds and advocate on behalf of libraries with local, state, and federal government. Friends groups continue to primarily be membership based, volunteer driven organizations, usually with federal 501(c)(3) tax exempt status. It varies from library to library whether or not the library's volunteer engagement coordinator has a liaison role to play with the Friends.

Many Friends of the Library groups find themselves facing serious issues—even extinction—as their active members age out and younger replacements are not recruited. This is often the case because they cling to outdated practices and old-fashioned volunteer management strategies.

The fund-raising and advocacy work of the Friends remains tremendously important to libraries. It's incumbent on the library, and on its staff liaison if structured that way, to recognize and embrace new trends in volunteerism. A shift from the old "volunteer management" to newer "volunteer engagement" practices is needed to accommodate the changing preferences of today's volunteers. The ability to attract the next generation of Friends depends on retooling their volunteer engagement efforts.

My own experience with joining Friends of the Library groups in two different states has been less than satisfying. After joining, the only communication I ever received was a periodic postcard in the mail inviting me to the Friends' book sale. The only connection I experienced with being a member was getting those postcards—and the chance to shop before the nonmembers. I was never asked or offered the opportunity to get involved in another way, so I felt little "ownership" of the organization or camaraderie with its members.

Although a key aspect of reviving Friends groups will be to retool their volunteer engagement practices to attract today's volunteers, it also seems that they often neglect current members, which is a lost opportunity. Susan Ellis, in her article "Make New Friends, But Keep the Old . . . ," discusses working with similar predominantly volunteer organizations such as fraternal organizations and service clubs: "All of these shared a common concern: recruiting new members. Why not start with the people already interested enough in the organization to remain on the membership rolls and pay dues?"[14]

Where to find more help in this book: Chapter 2, "Trend 1: Generational Differences" (p. 15), "Trend 2: Skilled Volunteers" (p. 19), and "Trend 3: Shift from Volunteer Management to Volunteer Engagement" (p. 20).

SUMMARY: ADDRESSING ISSUES AND PROBLEMS YOU MAY ENCOUNTER

There's not a problem you can describe that someone in the volunteer engagement game hasn't faced—ideas and answers are out there. Don't be paralyzed by fear of problems arising. If the task you need done will help people in your community and create a meaningful opportunity for a volunteer to become engaged and be transformed into a strong library supporter, it's definitely worth figuring out how to overcome the barriers to make it work.

NOTES

1. Campbell, Katherine Noyes, and Susan J. Ellis, *The (Help!) I-Don't-Have-Enough-Time Guide to Volunteer Management* (Philadelphia: Energize, 1995).
2. CharityLawyer, "Nonprofit Volunteers—Minimizing the Risks." http://charitylawyerblog.com/2013/01/23/nonprofit-volunteers-minimizing-the-risks-by-kimberly-witherspoon (accessed October 17, 2017).
3. Here are a few ideas for video clips to share:

"From Management to Engagement: Skilled Volunteers in Public Libraries" (1 hour archived webinar, September 2017). http://getinvolvedclearinghouse.org/resource/training-materials/management-engagement-skilled-volunteers-public-libraries (accessed October 11, 2017).

Interview with skilled volunteer Public Relations Specialist (2015). http://getinvolvedclearinghouse.org/resource/training-materials/skilled-volunteer-interview-public-relations-specialist (accessed October 11, 2017).

Interview with skilled volunteer Social Media Specialist (2015). http://getinvolvedca.org/resource/training-materials/skilled-volunteer-interview-social-media-specialist (accessed October 11, 2017).

Video clips on individual topics from a Get Involved Volunteer Engagement Institute (in Oakland, California, 2015):

"Benefits of Utilizing Skilled Volunteers at the Library," https://getinvolvedclearinghouse.org/resource/training-materials/benefits-using-skilled-volunteers-library (accessed February 22, 2018).

"Today's Volunteer: The Shift from Management to Engagement," https://getinvolvedclearinghouse.org/resource/training-materials/benefits-using-skilled-volunteers-library (accessed February 22, 2018).

"Importance of Meaningful Written Volunteer Job Descriptions," https://getinvolvedclearinghouse.org/resource/training-materials/importance-meaningful-written-volunteer-job-descriptions (accessed February 22, 2018).

4. Dixon, Andrea, and Melanie Hientz, "2013 Volunteer Recognition Study," Volunteer Canada, 2013. http://volunteer.ca/content/2013-volunteer-recognition-study (accessed June 15, 2017).

5. The Monrovia Public Library's Volunteer Management Team produced two brief videos totaling about 7 minutes describing their work and sharing their strategies and tips. They are available for viewing at http://www.getinvolvedca.org/resource/training-materials/meet-volunteer-management-team-monrovia-public-library-part-1 and http://www.getinvolvedca.org/resource/training-materials/volunteer-management-team-tips-and-strategies-monrovia-public-library (accessed October 11, 2017).

6. Type the word "teen" into the search feature of the Get Involved Clearinghouse for sample application, waiver, and consent forms, as well as sample job descriptions for teen volunteers: www.getinvolvedclearinghouse.org

7. Two YALSA wikis may be of some help: "Teen Volunteering & Service Projects," http://wikis.ala.org/yalsa/index.php/Teen_Volunteering_%26_Service_Projects and "Teen Advisory Groups," http://wikis.ala.org/yalsa/index.php/Teen_Advisory_Groups (both accessed October 23, 2017).

8. ASCLA, "Volunteers with Disabilities: What You Need to Know, Library Accessibility Tip Sheet 9." https://www.ascladirect.org/resources/volunteers-with-disabilities (accessed October 11, 2017).

9. Ibid.

10. More ASCLA tip sheets on specific accessibility issues can be found here: https://www.ascladirect.org/resources (accessed October 11, 2017).

11. Volunteering ACT, "Building Inclusive Bridges: A Guide to Facilitating Inclusive Referrals," 2016. https://www.volunteeringact.org.au/assets/publications/building-inclusive-bridges.pdf (accessed October 11, 2017).

12. "Inclusive Volunteering: Recommendations for Volunteer Coordinators on How to Develop a More Inclusive Volunteer Programme," 2015. http://dobrovolnickecentra.sk/subory/Recommendations_final.pdf (accessed October 11, 2017).

13. Reed, Sally Gardner, 2017 archived webinar, "Working with Friends Groups: The Good, the Great, and the Unfriendly." https://goo.gl/QsHUa6 (accessed October 18, 2017).

14. Ellis, Susan J., "Make New Friends but Keep the Old . . . ," 2007. https://energizeinc.com/hot-topics/2007/may (accessed October 18, 2017).

Resources

Volunteer engagement is a profession. Therefore, lots of people and materials are available to you. Here are some good places to begin to find what you need.

LOCAL VOLUNTEER SUPPORT ORGANIZATIONS

Your community may have one or more entire organizations such as Volunteer Centers and HandsOn Networks, which are in business to help you find volunteers, and some even provide training and support for staff who engage and support volunteers.

Your local United Way may also provide this service or be able to tell you who does in your area.

In addition, some communities have organized local professional associations for volunteer engagement professionals to meet periodically to share ideas and problem solve. Often called DOVIAs (Directors of Volunteers in Agencies), a list is maintained by state.[1]

Some city and county governments also offer volunteer recruitment services to their departments, so if your library is a part of your local government, be sure to participate where that is available. Examples include the city of Sacramento, California, and Washington County, Oregon.[2]

NATIONAL ORGANIZATIONS AND NETWORKS

A variety of national organizations and networks provide resources that may be of interest. Many offer webinars and other training opportunities, blogs, and links to other resources. Most also offer social media presence you can follow.

AL!VE: Association of Leaders in Volunteer Engagement

AL!VE—www.volunteeralive.org—is the national membership organization for professional volunteer resource managers. It strives to enhance and sustain the spirit of volunteerism by fostering collaboration and networking, promoting professional development, and providing advocacy for leaders in community engagement.

BoardSource

BoardSource's mission is to inspire and support excellence in nonprofit governance and board and staff leadership—https://boardsource.org. The resources provided for boards of all sizes may be very useful to your Board of Trustees, as well as to your Friends of the Library or Foundation board.

Corporation for National and Community Service

The Corporation for National and Community Service—www.nationalservice.gov—is the federal agency that helps millions of Americans improve the lives of their fellow citizens through service. They implement and oversee AmeriCorps, Senior Corps, Foster Grandparents, and FEMA Corps, as well as the national days of service—the Martin Luther King Jr. Day of Service and the September 11th National Day of Service and Remembrance.

In addition to grant information, their website delineates a number of special initiatives, as well as a digital repository of research, evaluation reports, and data focusing on national service, social innovation, civic engagement, and volunteering.

Serve.gov—www.serve.gov—a service of the Corporation, allows organizations to post volunteer opportunities for volunteers to find and express interest.

Council for Certification in Volunteer Administration

The mission of the council—www.cvacert.org—is to advance excellence in volunteer administration by delivering professional certification and advocating ethical practice. In addition to offering the CVA credential—Certified in Volunteer Administration—their commitment to excellence in the field includes a statement of Professional Ethics in Volunteer Management—http://cvacert.org/resources-and-media/professional-ethics.

Doing Good Together

Doing Good Together™ (DGT)—http://www.doinggoodtogether.org—is a Minneapolis-based national nonprofit that works to make volunteering and service, along with daily kindness, easy for every family. The organization offers opportunities for family volunteering and suggestions for acts of kindness and community service, each with reflections and book selections for a variety of age groups. Many tips, tools, and children's book lists are available for download, including suggestions for starting a Big-Hearted Family Book

Club. This site offers opportunities for libraries to introduce a new generation of families and children to community service and volunteer engagement.

Energize, Inc.

Although not a nonprofit organization, Energize, Inc.—https://energizeinc.com—offers a wealth of resources for those working in volunteer engagement. They are a major publisher and a seller of books and materials in the field, as well as a repository of training materials, conference and networking information, and an extensive online library of articles, book excerpts, free guides and reports, websites, blogs, and more.

LinkedIn Groups

Volunteer Coordinators: A place to network with other volunteer coordinators and managers, in addition to exchanging ideas and best practices related to the nonprofit sector. https://www.linkedin.com/groups/1911260.

Volunteer Management Best Practices Network: A network of administrators in the field of volunteer management to share resources, discuss best practices, engage in conversation, ask questions, and post interesting articles. https://www.linkedin.com/groups/3980663.

Virtual Volunteering: This forum encourages exchange of practical ideas related to doing or managing work done by volunteers online, via computer, smartphone, or other hand-held devices, often from a distance. https://www.linkedin.com/groups/6622229.

National Association of Volunteer Programs in Local Government

NAVPLG—www.navplg.org—is the national association of directors, managers, and administrators of volunteer programs in city, county, and other local governments. Its purpose is to strengthen volunteer programs through leadership, education, advocacy, networking, and information exchange.

NAVPLG focuses exclusively on the unique needs of volunteer programs within the structure of local governments.

Nonprofit Risk Management Center

The mission of the Nonprofit Risk Management Center—www.nonprofitrisk.org—is to enable nonprofit leaders to identify and manage risks that threaten their missions and operations, while empowering them to leverage opportunities and take bold, mission-advancing risks. In addition to training opportunities, publishing books on the subject, and a resource library on their website, the center offers VolunteerProtect!—a free mobile app that provides users with the full text of the Volunteer Protection Act of 1997, as well as specific state laws that provide protection from liability for volunteers. (Available for download in Google Play and the App store.)

Points of Light

Cast from the vision of 1,000 points of light shared by its founder President George H. W. Bush in his 1989 inaugural address, today Points of Light transcends politics and borders to inspire millions of volunteers worldwide. www.pointsoflight.org.

Working with corporate, nonprofit, and government partners, its goals are to mobilize people to take action to change the world, increase the impact of volunteers, leverage the power of volunteers to solve specific problems, and create a culture that supports and encourages more volunteers.

In addition to recognizing a "Daily Point of Light," nominated by community organizations, many resources on volunteer engagement are posted on their website, and All for Good—www.allforgood.org—a service of Points of Light, allows organizations to post volunteer opportunities for volunteers to find and express interest.

State Service Commissions

Each state has a state service commission that receives funds from the Corporation for National and Community Service to provide AmeriCorps and other grants to organizations within their states. Many also sponsor statewide volunteer awards and other initiatives that organizations may participate in. Find your state's commission here: https://www.nationalservice.gov/about/contact-us/state-service-commissions.

Virtual Volunteering Project

Operated by the RGK Center for Philanthropy and Community Service in the LBJ School of Public Affairs at the University of Texas at Austin, Serviceleader.org—www.serviceleader.org—provides information on volunteer engagement, recruiting, placing, supporting, and recognizing volunteers, as well as comprehensive resources in the area of virtual volunteering—https://www.serviceleader.org/virtual.

VolunteerMatch

In addition to its volunteer recruitment platform, VolunteerMatch offers free webinars, a blog, and other resources that can be found in their online Learning Center—http://learn.volunteermatch.org. You can also watch for upcoming events and new resources by following them on Facebook or Twitter.

LIBRARY-SPECIFIC VOLUNTEERISM RESOURCES

Get Involved Clearinghouse: www.getinvolvedclearinghouse.org

The Get Involved Clearinghouse is a searchable database of materials shared by libraries participating in the Get Involved: Powered by Your Library initiative. Begun as a California statewide initiative designed to expand the visibility and contributions of skilled volunteers through public libraries, its success led to a three-year grant to a collaborative of four state library agencies—Arizona, California, Idaho, and Texas—from the Institute for Museum and Library Services' Laura Bush 21st Century Librarian Program.

Resources are categorized under "Management Tools" (forms, handbooks, etc.), "Position Descriptions" (skilled volunteer job description ideas), and "Training Materials" (including both training outlines and videotaped training pieces on a variety of topics). Each category includes a keyword dropdown menu to help narrow your search. Materials may be downloaded to help create local versions that suit your needs.

LinkedIn Group: Library Volunteer Administrators

A group for anyone who oversees or supervises volunteers in a library setting: https://www.linkedin.com/groups/4353796.

United for Libraries—http://www.ala.org/united

This is the Association of Library Trustees, Advocates, Friends, and Foundations. Their mission is to support those who govern, promote, advocate, and fund-raise for all types of libraries. United for Libraries offers a variety of resources of interest to library support organizations. An item of particular interest may be "Libraries Need Friends: A Toolkit to Create Friends Groups or to Revitalize the Ones You Have." http://www.ala.org/united/sites/ala.org.united/files/content/friends/libraries-need-friends.pdf.

RESOURCES FOR VOLUNTEERS WITH SPECIAL NEEDS

"Inclusive Volunteering: Recommendations for Volunteer Coordinators on How to Develop a More Inclusive Volunteer Programme"[3] is a 2016 publication prepared as part of a two-year project, Volunteering as a Tool for Inclusion (2013–2015), carried out by eight partner organizations from Croatia, Denmark, Hungary, Ireland, Italy, Latvia, Romania, and Slovakia.

It provides overall guidance as well as specific suggestions for working with volunteers with hearing or visual impairments, physical disabilities, mental health difficulties, and volunteers on the autism spectrum, as well as those who are older, migrants, unemployed, ex-prisoners, or homeless.

ANNOTATED BIBLIOGRAPHY OF BOOKS

Burych, Christine, Alison Caird, Joanne Fine Schwebel, Michael Fliess, and Heather Hardie, *Measuring the Impact of Volunteers: A Balanced and Strategic Approach* (Philadelphia: Energize Books, 2016).

By describing an alternative to the traditional metrics of reporting volunteer service—"by the numbers"—this book shows you how to help reflect the true value of volunteers to your organization. Those familiar with the balanced scorecard measurement tool first developed by Kaplan and Norton in the 1990s will recognize the concepts adapted uniquely for volunteer involvement.

Campbell, Katherine Noyes, and Susan J. Ellis, *The (Help!) I-Don't-Have-Enough-Time Guide to Volunteer Management* (Philadelphia: Energize Books, 1995).

Written for volunteer engagement leaders who are stretched thin—struggling to handle the demands of creating and running volunteer projects as an adjunct to other job responsibilities or on a part-time basis—this book offers valuable tips for time management.

Ellis, Susan, *From the Top Down: The Executive Role in Volunteer Program Success*, 3rd ed. (Philadelphia: Energize, March 2010).

Written for the top level decision maker—executive director, library director, etc.—this book focuses on key aspects for ensuring success, from staffing, budgeting, and legal issues, to determining dollar value of volunteers and evaluating impact.

Ellis, Susan, and Katherine Noyes Campbell, *Proof Positive: Developing Significant Volunteer Record-Keeping Systems,* 21st century ed. (Philadelphia: Energize, 2003).

Create your own forms from many samples; collect and communicate volunteer information in easy and effective ways; write reports that get your executive's attention.

Fixler, Jill Friedman, et al., *Boomer Volunteer Engagement: Collaborate Today, Thrive Tomorrow* (Bloomington, IN: AuthorHouse, 2008).

The authors present a step-by-step process for creating a culture for boomer volunteers to thrive in your organization.

Graff, Linda, *Better Safe: Risk Management in Volunteer Programs and Community Service* (Canada: Graff and Associates, 2003).

A definitive work on a sensitive but vital subject. Screening volunteers (and employees) has always been an important part of the volunteer coordinator's job, but in today's climate of risk and liability, the stakes have risen considerably.

Herman, Melanie L., *No Surprises: Harmonizing Risk and Reward in Volunteer Management,* 5th ed. (Washington, D.C.: The Nonprofit Risk Management Center, 2009).

Clear, easy-to-read book that demystifies risk management and explains this responsibility for directors of volunteers in any setting. Learn how to limit risk at each step of managing a volunteer program.

Holt, Glen E., and Leslie Edmonds Holt, *Success with Library Volunteers* (Santa Barbara, CA: Libraries Unlimited, 2013).

Two library practitioners address operational realities and will help library leaders who are just beginning, or who are revising their approach to volunteer engagement.

Kelly, Colleen, and Lynda Gerty, *The Abundant Not-for-Profit: How Talent (Not Money) Will Transform Your Organization* (Canada: Vantage Point, 2013). http://www.thevantagepoint.ca/abundant-not-profit-book.

Inspiration and practical ideas to help you think beyond scarcity and step up to the challenge of engaging educated, experienced, and talented people in the work of your organization.

Lee, Jarene Frances, with Julia M. Catagnus, *What We Learned (the Hard Way) about Supervising Volunteers* (Philadelphia: Energize, 1999).

Advice, wisdom, and experience from more than 85 real-life, on-the-job supervisors of volunteers. A good analysis of what works and what doesn't work in supervision.

Lehn, Carla Campbell, *Volunteer Involvement in California Libraries: Best Practices* (Sacramento: California State Library, 1999). https://getinvolvedclearinghouse.org/resource/training-materials/volunteer-involvement-california-libraries-best-practices

Based on the experiences of the author's work with library volunteer programs, this book describes the critical elements for volunteer program success and provides sample materials that can be used to further develop a library volunteer program.

Rosenthal, Robert J., Ed., *Volunteer Engagement 2.0: Ideas and Insights Changing the World* (Hoboken, NJ: Wiley & Sons, 2015).

Explores the innovative volunteer engagement approaches that are reshaping nonprofits and their communities, and shows how you can bring these approaches to your own organization. The chapter on "Leading Big Volunteer Operations" is a case study of the California State Library's own "Get Involved: Powered by Your Library" statewide initiative.

Smallwood, Carol, and Lura Sanborn, Eds., *Library Volunteers Welcome! Strategies for Attracting, Retaining and Making the Most of Willing Helpers* (Jefferson, NC: McFarland & Company, 2016).

This collection of 30 new essays (including three by Carla Campbell Lehn) brings together the experiences of numerous individuals across the United States, providing ideas, projects, and best practices in five sections: recruitment and retention; policies and process; mentoring and empowering; placement programs and responsibilities; and outreach.

Stallings, Betty, with Susan Ellis, *Leading the Way to Successful Volunteer Involvement: Practical Tools for Busy Executives* (Philadelphia: Energize, 2010).

Central to this book is the belief that the key factor in volunteer success is the attention of an organization's top decision makers. Each section sequentially moves through a strategic volunteer engagement planning process. From budgeting for volunteer engagement, through ensuring legal compliance and managing risk, the book provides insights and tools to help.

Volunteer Centre Dacorum, *A Toolkit for Volunteer Speed Matching* (Philadelphia: Energize, 2005).

A clever volunteer center in London created a "Volunteer Speed Matching" event with all the characteristics of speed dating including score sheets, a stop watch, and "daters" moving from table to table on 3-minute whistle sounds! They produced this toolkit with event planning tips, templates for score sheets and other basic materials, sample press releases, etc.

Wall, Milan, and Vicki Luther, *10 Ideas for Recruiting New Leaders* (Lincoln, NE: Heartland Center for Leadership Development, (800) 927–1115, 2000).

Ten excellent ideas based on actions of community leaders dealing with the very real problem of developing new leadership.

Wilson, Marlene, *Visionary Leadership in Volunteer Programs: Insights* (Philadelphia: Energize, 2008).

A collection of favorite and most-requested presentations from Marlene Wilson, volunteer management pioneer and leader in the field.

SUMMARY

You are not alone! The field of volunteer engagement is filled with research, resources, networks, and practitioners who want to help you succeed. So, don't be shy—get out there and find your local and national networks—or if there is no local network where you live and work, create one! Volunteer engagement coordinators in a variety of nonprofits and community organizations in your geographic area are also probably feeling isolated and would love to get together periodically for discussion and support—they're just waiting for someone to call!

NOTES

1. Energize Inc. www.energizeinc.com/prof/dovia.html (accessed March 30, 2017).
2. City of Sacramento (CA): http://www.cityofsacramento.org/HR/Volunteer-Opportunities (accessed March 12, 2017). Washington County (OR) Volunteer Links: http://www.co.washington.or.us/Volunteers/Volunteer-Links.cfm (accessed March 12, 2017).
3. "Inclusive Volunteering: Recommendations for Volunteer Coordinators on How to Develop a More Inclusive Volunteer Programme." http://dobrovolnickecentra.sk/subory/Recommendations_final.pdf (accessed September 23, 2017).

Index

About the Author

CARLA CAMPBELL LEHN, principal consultant of the Lehn Group, is a former library programs consultant at the California State Library, where she worked on literacy, rural, and community engagement initiatives, including the design of the statewide library volunteerism initiative *Get Involved: Powered by Your Library*. She began her career as a VISTA volunteer, and spent a number of years with United Way after that. Recently retired from the state library, she's spending time again on her consulting practice, doing some bucket list travel, and continuing to serve as an active Girl Scout volunteer. Connect with her at *https://www.linkedin.com/in/carlalehn*.